DOORS OPEN
TORONTO

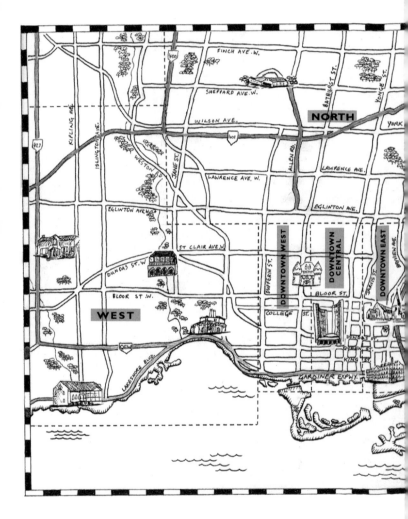

DOORS OPEN TORONTO

EAST

DON MILLS RD.

VICTORIA PARK AVE.

KENNEDY RD.

McGOWAN RD.

MARKHAM RD.

FINCH AVE. E.

SHEPPARD AVE. E.

MORNINGSIDE AVE.

ELLESMERE RD.

DVP

LAWRENCE AVE. E.

EGLINTON AVE. E.

VICTORIA PARK AVE.

DANFORTH RD.

O'CONNOR DR.

KINGSTON RD.

...RTH AVE.

GERRARD ...

DUNDAS ST. E.

LAKE ONTARIO

DOORS
OPEN
TORONTO

ILLUMINATING THE CITY'S
GREAT SPACES

JOHN SEWELL

ALFRED A. KNOPF CANADA

PUBLISHED BY ALFRED A. KNOPF CANADA

National Library of Canada Cataloguing in Publication Data

Sewell, John, 1940–
Doors open Toronto : illuminating the city's great spaces

Includes index.
ISBN 0-676-97498-8

1. Historic buildings–Ontario–Toronto–Guidebooks. 2. Toronto
(Ont.)–Buildings, structures, etc.–Guidebooks. 3. Toronto
(Ont.)–Guidebooks. 4. Toronto (Ont.)–History. I. Title.

FC3097.7.S49 2002   917.13'41044   C2002-900398-9
F1059.5.T688A2 2002

Grateful acknowledgment is made to
Michael Ondaatje for permission to reprint from *In the Skin of a Lion*.
(McClelland & Stewart: Toronto, 1987)

Pages 266 to 269 constitute a continuation of the copyright page.

First Edition

www.randomhouse.ca

Printed and bound in Canada

2 4 6 8 9 7 5 3

With great affection and admiration for my parents,
Helen and Bill Sewell,
both of whom died in their mid-nineties
after long and fruitful lives,
in the latter months of 2001, as
I was writing this book.

CONTENTS

DOWNTOWN: EAST

DOWNTOWN: WEST

EAST

NORTH

WEST

FOREWORD

Where Once We Dwelled

L ong before, and long after, I imagined undressing the city as one undresses a lover: each time differently. In the city's creases—the ravines, the twenty streams, the folds of the escarpment—a lifetime of desire slipped into laneways and cafés, like prayers slipped between the stones of a temple.

I imagined offering you secret places, discovered during years of solitary rambling; the fragment of stonework revealed only in winter light, the abandoned bank crumbling over the edge of a cliff. Like falling from love-at-first-sight into love, we would descend, float from the street to the floor of the ravine, to the downtown stream I swam in as a girl, office buildings looming around us. The immense marble cave of a night lobby, glowing with all the dim radiance of hundreds of square feet of pressurized limestone. The massive two-storey wooden doors, each iron hinge the size of a child. All the hidden hydro houses surreptitiously slipped into neighbourhoods, with their impeccable lawns and tasteful blinds hiding pulsing megawatts of raw power. The factory tower too well constructed to be (cost-effectively) torn down, standing alone in a parking lot like a ten-storey idol facing the sea. The stone books. The secret places in the city to watch the trains at dusk, or to watch the moon rise, its pale light across the lake like the line of skin revealed under a sweater as an arm reaches over-head, the quietness of that gaze. The perfect inch of city, a glimpse squeezed between two stores. The tenderness of privet hedges, meticulously trimmed, surrounding the abandoned ruins of the detergent factory. All the secrets of Sunlight Park Road.

In night stories, just before sleep, you talked of places that disap-peared before we met, places you lived, no longer even ruins or rem-nants, now just a slant of light. You recounted all the trespassing you did as a boy, all the neighbourhood fences you climbed, dropping silent as a thief into dark summer yards. The same hours I was slipping into the same night. Both of us searching for the same city.

This city, this body, where once we dwelled.

Every city, no matter how modern or ancient, populous or abandoned, is saturated with eros.

The built world is where geologic and human memory meet, like fate and free will.

Every building is an intersection, where one's experience meets the experience of others, where the past lives in the present, Walter Benjamin's "waking world toward which the past is dreaming": the confusion of song in a synagogue that was once a Baptist church; the converted bakery–factory, tenants living where cakes were once decorated, the smell of fresh bread sabotaging their thoughts.

The city is alive with places we will never see inside of—both present places and lost places (lost possibilities) that continue to live their ghostly absence inside the same space as new buildings, or in the empty air of parking lots.

This eros that floods Toronto streets, the city built in the ancient lake bed; this eros of place never owned yet wholly inhabited.

———

One weekend a year, Toronto opens its doors. Churches, mosques, theatres, the legislature, the old post office, factories, office towers, breweries, the Necropolis cemetery . . .

The city is a body, with its hidden histories, with its structures and infrastructures, and for two days we have a chance to take a good look at who we are; all that a building can teach us—not only about its own usefulness and all that has gone on inside it and continues to, but about those who designed it and those who built it, about the local and not-so-local materials it's made from and the memory of the site itself. Every building, like every human, represents its times, its context. How beautiful the proximity of the old city hall and the new; what clearer example of the defining spirits of two different eras, cleaving to each other as eras do, each made more itself by the presence and proximity of the other.

Every building is a monument to hope; a huge commitment of purpose, of commerce, of community, of an aesthetic, of continued human engagement: in every way a statement of its time.

I long for the Georgian Toronto I never knew, and for the Georgian Toronto I knew. I miss the cottages on Elizabeth Street, on Boulton

Street, which is now Pearl, on Gerrard Street where even the chestnut trees that once gave their shade are no longer. I resent the fire that consumed the Yorkville Town Hall with its Flemish facade, long before I was born.

Whatever happened to the huge golden griffin that guarded the "great silk and clothing house" on King Street? Where is the Glaswegian coat of arms, cut from stone, that once graced Robert Marshall's Bookstore, also on King Street, and where are Robert Marshall's books now?

Perhaps such "ornaments" are unimportant. But the lessons and losses all buildings teach us are not.

A building may outlast us, but it also may not—no matter how grand or monumental, how ornate, how seemingly essential in purpose and place. Not to mention the tiny café where old friends married twenty years ago; or the converted storefront and all its subsequent cafés, where friends sat so happily one particular winter morning: only their conversation remains.

———

What factory believes it will become bedrooms? What bank believes it will someday bake cakes? What refinery believes someone will care enough to surround its ruins with the sweetness of a garden?

Every building holds such possibility, many possible incarnations. Perhaps that is our sorrow in seeing a building abandoned, or disregarded, in ruins; a betrayal that is almost always human. There is a way in which a building keeps believing, long after there is no hope left.

At first, nothing seems so closed as a fact. The facts of a life. The facts of a building that has known only one existence, a building so overlooked it cannot imagine anyone eager to look inside. But every fact is a door.

———

One rainy morning, stand outside the gate of Osgoode Hall and look down the street along the magnificent black wrought-iron fence designed by William Storm, once a newly arrived four-year-old immigrant boy from Lincolnshire, who gave so much of his imagination to this city. In a lost November twilight visit the luxurious austerity of the seminary of St. Augustine's or the R. C. Harris Filtration Plant.

Drink midnight tea on the winter lawn of Berkeley Castle, on a clean white cloth of snow hidden from the street. Then, on one rare weekend in May, when the "Doors Open," go back to these places and look inside. . . .

The most important doors open very rarely. If a city opens its doors, don't hesitate on the threshold. Walk through.

PREFACE

T oronto has more than its own fair share of intriguing stories that illuminate the past and explain the present, and many of those stories are in the city's structures. That's one of the key ideas behind Doors Open Toronto: those who look closely at the city's buildings will gain a better appreciation of the city itself.

But maintaining the presence of the past is not easy. Little legislative protection is available for buildings, and it is a constant struggle to convince governments and building owners that structures should be enhanced and retained rather than demolished. The many individuals who stick up for existing buildings in the face of some new vision of a "better" future deserve our thanks and support. A walk down virtually any street will confirm that older buildings are usually more interesting and felicitous than newer ones. Not always, of course: sometimes architects of our own time are given the scope of designing structures that are equal to the best of the past. But too often fine older buildings are demeaned by the inferior design and quality of what has arrived since they were built.

The Doors Open idea came to Toronto in the simplest of ways. Catherine Nasmith, an architect with a serious interest in heritage issues, had had many discussions with a distant relative living in Edinburgh, Sir James Dunbar-Nasmith, CBE. Sir James was chair of the Scottish Civic Trust, and his involvement in the preservation movement meant he was part of the Doors Open idea, which Glasgow had latched on to in 1990, with Edinburgh joining the following year. Doors Open had started in a small town in France in 1984 and had been gathering momentum ever since. By 1991 it was a weekend event in eleven European cities. By 1998 some nineteen million visitors had visited twenty-eight thousand sites in forty-four countries, operating under the name European Heritage Days. The model was simple: open buildings for a day or a weekend (never longer), and tell the public they're welcome to visit.

Catherine Nasmith invited Sir James, who was in Toronto in August 1998 on a social visit, to speak about his experience with Doors Open. More than a hundred people attended what was to have been an informal event. Karen Black—now of the City of Toronto Culture Division, then of Heritage Toronto—was knocked out by the idea, and started the program here. Toronto became the first city in North America to launch Doors Open. In 1999 Catherine Nasmith was appointed to the board of Heritage Toronto, and the decision was made to send an exploratory group to Glasgow and Edinburgh. The group consisted of Karen Black and her colleague Jane French, Margie Zeidler, Catherine Nasmith, and Michael and Anne Tippin. On their return, the steering committee and City staff decided to hold the first Doors Open in Toronto in May 2000, with the theatre entrepreneur David Mirvish as the honorary patron. With nearly one hundred buildings participating and over seventy thousand visitors, it was an enormous success. To date it continues to attract many thousands of people

Doors Open Toronto has quickly grown into a popular event because people are curious about buildings and their history. This book makes a start in helping that process, trying to place buildings in a social, physical, and political context. The more people learn, the better they will understand why Toronto is not quite the same as other places but embodies its own set of values and styles. The more they discover about the city, the greater the chance they will participate in creating its future. What Toronto needs is a host of informed citizens ready to stand up for a vision of the city that brings into daily life more social equity, more beauty, and more sense of the past. That will come as people are given the opportunity to brush up against the past in their daily lives and as they connect with others to realize that acting together they can have a serious and positive influence on the life of the city and its residents. At the end of the day, an understanding and appreciation of the past is the best hope we have for a better present and future. Doors Open Toronto plays an important role in that process.

Of course, there are many resources to turn to once this small book and the buildings it discusses have been exhausted. A starting list of useful books can be found at the end of this one.

DOWNTOWN: CENTRAL

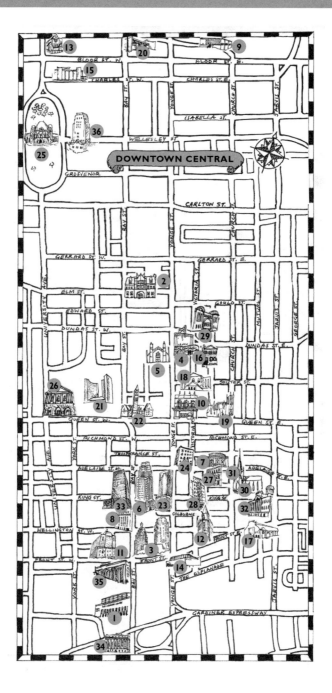

DOWNTOWN CENTRAL

AIR CANADA CENTRE

40 Bay Street

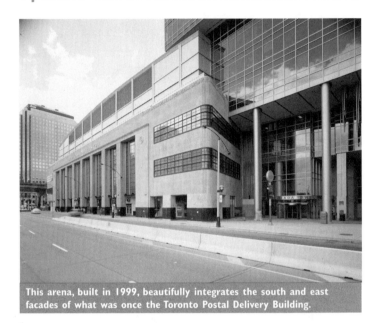

This arena, built in 1999, beautifully integrates the south and east facades of what was once the Toronto Postal Delivery Building.

The Air Canada Centre, opened in February 1999, is one of the city's best examples of the way an important architectural masterpiece can be rehabilitated for another use.

In the late 1930s the government of Canada commissioned the architect Charles Dolphin to design a new postal facility for Toronto. He created the Toronto Postal Delivery Building, constructed between 1939 and 1941. The south facade, under the grimy gloom of the Gardiner Expressway, best reflects the original design. The bottom six feet of the building are dressed in polished black granite. Each wide fluted pillar runs cleanly toward the roof, and between them are large multi-paned window bays. The top and edges of the facade are Queenston limestone. Marching along the roofline are two Canadian icons—maple leaves and beavers chewing on stumps.

The Bay Street facade has been renovated and changed in a very interesting manner. The black polished granite continues at the base of each pillar, but the lower portion of each window bay has been cut away, opening, behind the pillars, to a protected walkway providing relief from the noise of the busy street traffic. It is a very elegant variation that takes nothing away from Dolphin's design, influenced by the German Bauhaus movement, emphasizing simple, clean lines and clarity of form. The Toronto architecture firm Brisbin Brook Beynon are to be commended in their sensitive reworking of Dolphin's scheme.

The real surprise on the exterior is the bas-reliefs, tracing the history of communication. The story starts at the northeast corner of the building, just above the polished black marble: the carving shows cavemen calling out to each other, followed by a man beating on a hollow log, then a man carrying a written message in a stick. The story continues at the southeast corner, with Indians sending smoke signals, a mail coach fending off attacks as it lurches through the desert, coureurs de bois navigating Canadian waterways by canoe, and a team of huskies running through the snow. At the southwest corner, the first carving is of a postman delivering mail, followed by a transport plane that appears capable of landing on water, a cargo ship, a sailing ship in full gear, and a steam locomotive.

The new arena has been carefully fitted within the east and south walls. The main access is cleverly designed through a gallery between the railway tracks and the arena itself, above which is a twelve-storey office tower, mostly occupied by Air Canada. At the east end of this large and commodious gallery are artifacts from Dolphin's original

One of the many limestone bas-relief carvings that grace the facades, tracing the history of human communication.

structure, including the elegant Art Deco lettering from the building's sign, a large copper coat of arms, and another section of chewing beavers that, being displayed at eye level, can be inspected and admired. Off the gallery are shops, restaurants, and a direct connection to Union Station.

The entrance to the arena is on the south side of the gallery. The arena itself is designed to accommodate hockey as a first preference—seating 18,800—but can easily be modified for the Toronto Raptors basketball team and music concerts, adding 1,000 seats. Unlike some contemporary arenas that fans complain lack character and atmosphere, the ACC is compact, creating that happy feeling of each spectator being comfortably part of a crowd, with reasonable proximity to the playing surface. The ceiling is hung with appropriate pennants reflecting the history of the Toronto Maple Leafs, first established as a hockey team in the 1920s, and the more recent Toronto Raptors. Regular tours of the Air Canada Centre are held on a daily basis, providing access to dressing rooms, the Esso Maple Leafs' Memory and Dreams Room, with interactive displays, and other behind-the-scene areas.

Outside, immediately to the west of the ACC, is the enormous sculpture by John McEwen, consisting of three large metal tubes pierced with stars, appearing to offer views of either distant galaxies or spaces within the earth. It is titled *Search Light, Star Light and Spot Light*.

Artifacts and signage from the 1939 post office, in the gallery leading into the Air Canada Centre.

ARTS AND LETTERS CLUB

14 Elm Street

This red-stone and-brick structure may seem reminiscent of Dutch and North German architecture, but it was built for the St. George's Society in 1891 to encourage British traditions in Canada. The Society fell on hard times, and in 1920 the Arts and Letters Club moved in, leaving the St. George's name carved in stone above the main entrance.

Behind the strong oak doors, up a few steps, and through the corridor is the extraordinary baronial hall, with wood panelling, choir gallery, fireplace, and heraldic crests. The hall was created in the Tudor manner by the local architectural partnership of Sproatt & Rolph, retained in 1920 to remodel the interior when the Arts and Letters Club took over. This firm had recently completed Hart House, on the University of Toronto campus, and similarities exist between the design of its Great Hall and this space.

The Arts and Letters Club was founded in 1909, for men only. Its original quarters were in the York County Court House on Adelaide Street, where it remained for a decade before moving to and renting the Elm Street premises for sixty-six years, finally purchasing the property in 1986. The club had become a centre of activity for musicians, writers, theatre people, and artists, including some of the painters who would in 1920 form the Group of Seven.

Women were first allowed to be present at a Club function in this room in 1921. Nellie McClung, the women's advocate (she was elected to the Legislative Assembly in Alberta in 1921), gave a speech before famous Canadian women of the day, among them Lucy Maud Montgomery (author of the *Anne of Green Gables* books). The year 1921 was a critical one for women in Canada—they were finally permitted to vote, and Agnes McPhail was the first woman elected to

The insignia above, designed in 1909 by J. E. H. MacDonald, a member of the Group of Seven and for some years president of the Arts and Letters Club, has served as the Club's crest for nearly a century. C. W. Jefferys, another artist and former Club president, described the insignia as "the Viking ship with sails full spread before the rising sun," reminding members "of the open sea and the great adventure."

Parliament. Also in McClung's audience was Emily Pankhurst, the English suffragist, who, as Greg Gatenby writes in *Toronto: A Literary Guide*, "happened to be in town." Gatenby also notes that many other famous persons spoke in the Club, including A. A. Milne (author of *Winnie the Pooh*), John Buchan (the writer and later a governor general), G. K. Chesterton, and the Canadian poets Bliss Carman and Duncan Campbell Scott. Today, the Club has undergone something of a rejuvenation, again becoming an important venue for a variety of cultural events, with a lively membership.

Many drawings and paintings from the first half of the twentieth century, mostly by the Group of Seven and their followers, grace hallways and various meeting rooms throughout the building. The Great Hall still features lunches and dinners, debates and discussion, and exhibitions.

The Club's baronial dining hall.

BCE PLACE

181 Bay Street

The Galleria takes pedestrians past the facade of a Toronto bank designed by William Thomas, the same architect responsible for the old Don Jail and St. Lawrence Hall.

BCE Place (the initials reflect the name of Bell Canada Enterprises, a company now operating much more than mere telephone service) occupies virtually the whole block bounded by Bay, Wellington, Yonge, and Front Streets. Designed in 1990 by the Toronto architects Bregman and Hamann, with the famous American firm Skidmore, Owings & Merrill as consultants, it's an odd duck of a development, consisting of remnants of the old among the new, and an extraordinary example of interior urban design.

BCE Place was one of the first projects to reflect a return to the principles of an earlier cityscape. To begin with, BCE Place is built right out to the street line for most of its perimeter, in contrast to the dominant practice from the 1960s through the '80s of setting tall buildings well back on vast empty plazas, like the Toronto Dominion Centre and Commerce Court. BCE Place's Yonge Street frontage incorporates several four-storey structures from the nineteenth century, which give a good sense of what the older city must have felt like. Unfortunately, only facades remain: street access to the buildings has been abandoned to accommodate the late-twentieth-century custom of channelling street activity into interior malls, as has been done in the Eaton Centre, a half dozen blocks to the north.

These historical facades on Yonge Street, dating back to the mid-1800s, are elements of the few buildings in the area to survive the Great Fire of 1904.

The street level of BCE Place contains an elliptical vaulted glass atrium that functions as an interior pedestrian way, designed by the Spanish architect Santiago Calatrava. Light plays magically through the steel-and-glass canopy covering this welcoming space. To the north of the walkway is a small exhibit area adjacent to the elevators, where uninspired pen-and-ink portraits of influential business leaders are found, accompanied by an explanation of their commercial acumen.

The south side of the walkway shows the remains of the Midland Commercial Bank building. Constructed in the 1840s on Wellington Street just west of Yonge, it was by the 1960s owned by Clarkson Gordon, a firm headed by the former federal minister of finance Walter Gordon. As he was writing the foreword to Eric Arthur's classic book on the city's architecture, *Toronto, No Mean City*, Gordon learned

The dramatic stonework of the former Bank of Montreal gives a monumental feel to the Hockey Hall of Fame.

that substantial renovations were required or the building would have to be demolished. He decided he owed it to Arthur to renovate the whole building, which he did. But two decades later it was neverthe-less mostly demolished, and its facade was moved several hundred feet south to accommodate the two new towers of BCE Place. The honey-coloured limestone facade of the Greek Revival bank continues to be very satisfying visually.

Much of the exterior of the BCE Place complex gives no hint of its interior interest, and the two aluminium-and-glass towers end high in the sky in a chubby tiered fashion. A more pleasing view may be the Dominion Building across Front Street, running from Bay to Yonge, with its gently curved facade and its solidly comforting stonework, including beavers lounging above the doors.

On the northwest corner of Front and Yonge Streets is a former Bank of Montreal, built in 1885. As the journalist and critic Robert Fulford notes in his book *Accidental City*, the architect Frank Darling "made it an exuberantly rococo celebration of an expanding nation...[with] a blizzard of visual allegories spelled out in stone and stained glass." Sadly, like its neighbours to the north, this building is no longer accessible from the street, as it was designed to be. Now part of the Hockey Hall of Fame, mainly located in the underground mall, the bank has its win-dows blocked with team insignia. The current use has overwhelmed the structure, whose fine stained-glass skylight and wooden panelling are only incidental backdrops to the Hall of Fame experience.

CANON THEATRE
(FORMERLY THE PANTAGES)

🚪 244 Victoria Street

Entering the doors under the modest marquee on Yonge Street presents the visitor with a glittering entrance way to the Canon Theatre. Like that of other theatres in Toronto, the entrance may be on the main street, but the theatre itself is on a street to the rear, and patrons are enticed inside by a beguiling transition.

Here the hallway ceiling is a riot of colours, arranged in designs reminiscent of ancient Greek ones, and that theme is picked out in one of the paintings, showing two women admiring the statue of a Greek man at sunset. The mirrors on the walls sparkle and are set off by dark blue curtains. A series of marble steps lifts theatregoers over the hidden laneway to the mezzanine lobby of the theatre.

This oval room is a comfortable container for a crowd—no corners—and the shape is emphasized by the large recessed ceiling design, centred with a chandelier and surrounded by sixteen roundels. The artist is unknown, but the bas-relief plaster Greek figures contained within the roundels are of an exceptionally high quality, and their modest cream and green colours give them no prominence in this space, which is overloaded with attractions for the eye. Around the walls are dark blue fluted columns, mirrors in gilt frames, and drinking fountains under scalloped arches. The balcony railing is man-made scagliola, not marble. A handsome staircase curves from the mezzanine to the main floor, allowing excellent opportunities to see and be seen. The painting above the stairway is undistinguished—rumour is that the women in the original painting have been slimmed down by the hands of more recent artists. On the south side of the lobby is a large bar, not present in the 1920s when the theatre was built, because of prohibition. At that time this area opened directly into the rear of the theatre.

Entering the theatre, one is presented with a very strong statement. The seats are a dignified blue, set off nicely by the beige walls and brass railings. The proscenium around the stage is covered in decoration, and to either side are boxes, from which columns rise to support large gilt filigree panels, apparently showing winged figures in a forest. Many who have seen performances here are not familiar with the rather extravagant

Inside the Canon Theatre is a breathtaking ceiling dome, covered during the long-running Pantages show The Phantom of the Opera.

decoration—it was blacked out for *The Phantom of the Opera*, which was resident for more than a decade. On the ceiling is a magnificent dome in black, mauve, and gold leaf, the black mesh portion hiding the organ room in the Pantages, as the theatre was called when it first opened. At the back, over the gently sloping balcony, are shallow domes with chandeliers thought to be originals. The theatre comfortably seats more than twenty-two hundred on two levels.

This theatre was originally called the Pantages, after Pericles Alexander Pantages, an American who, in trying to join the gold rush in the Yukon, became part owner of a saloon staging burlesque shows in the early twentieth century. From there he moved into films and took control of 120 theatres across North America. Most were called the Pantages. In 1929 he was convicted of raping a young chorus girl, and although that conviction was overturned on appeal, he never recovered and was forced to sell his chain.

The structure was originally built for vaudeville in 1920, and designed by Thomas Lamb. After 1930, renamed the Imperial, it was used only for films. In 1973 the building was remodelled by the late Toronto architect Mandel Sprachman into six small movie theatres, called the Imperial Six. In 1986 a legal fight developed between Canada's two large theatre chains, and the courts issued an injunction that the site could never again be used for films. The decision was made to convert it to a theatre, and Sprachman was once again called in. His touch had been sensitive enough in 1973 that in 1989 he was able to easily convert the space to a glorious theatre that resembles Lamb's original.

The lobby.

CHURCH OF THE HOLY TRINITY

10 Trinity Square

Most Anglican churches built in the first half of the nineteenth century were funded by people who had done well financially, with little thought to social needs or the poor. In contrast, the Church of the Holy Trinity was the result of a donation from one Mary Swale of Yorkshire, England, of what today would represent

$1 million for "the erection of a church in the diocese of Toronto to be called the Church of the Holy Trinity; the seats of which were to be free and unappropriated for ever," writes William Dendy in *Toronto Observed*.

Henry Bowyer Lane, of English background but with a successful Toronto practice, architect of St. George's Anglican Church and Little Trinity Church, also designed Holy Trinity in 1847. The building is yellow brick, with two stone courses below the Gothic arched windows separated by simple brick piers. The footprint (or shape if viewed from above) is a Latin cross, with large windows terminating all four arms. The main formal entrance is on the western face (the day-to-day entrance is on the south side), and there are several decorations: lovely leafy carvings and medallions at the upper edges of the door, a small stretch of crenellation above the door, carved stone heads at the ends of the Gothic wishbone around the upper window, and a railing on the slopes of the roof. Unlike most churches, this one has no tower, although two turrets one could expect to find on a castle rise on either side of the main door, echoed by smaller turrets just behind them. Under the eaves at the perimeter of the roof are many plaques, kings' heads, and Masonic symbols ringing the building. In sum, the exterior is plain and straight-forward with pleasant decorative surprises.

The interior is unusual: it is a large auditorium without columns to create nave and aisles. The variety in style of the colourful and large stained windows is extraordinary: traditional patterns, patterns enhanced by paint, classical figures, and non-figurative motifs. Those on the south wall were done by Stephen Taylor in 1982. The windows over the altar at the east end of the church—made in Edinburgh in 1858—show the four Evangelists above and four prophets below. A sumptuous wooden choir screen hides the legs of the prophets. The decoration on the wooden altar alternates between sturdy columns and delicate tracery. The wooden pulpit on the left side of the chancel sits on three columns, a reference to the Trinity in the church's name. The ceiling is covered in a painted stencilled floral design in two shades of Wedgwood blue, high-lighted by bursts of rose and occasional white doves. There is a very interesting baptismal font dating from 1847 at the right of the chancel. Rather than fixed pews, movable benches ensure there is no sense of ownership in seating arrangements.

When the Eaton Centre was first proposed in the mid-1960s, it called for the demolition of the Church of the Holy Trinity, but the congregation fought long and hard to preserve it. Trinity Square had been joined to Yonge Street by a short roadway that was ultimately closed off and the mall built over it, and the main entryway is now from Bay Street. The two church houses that once stood on Trinity Square were moved to their present location just to the east of the church, up against the Eaton Centre wall. It was in one of these structures—at 6 Trinity Square—that Henry Scadding, the first rector of Holy Trinity, wrote his famous history *Toronto of Old*.

In negotiations with the Eaton Centre developers, the congregation managed to secure an appropriate sum of money to renovate the church and to pursue the social programs that have been such a strong part of the church's life. One happy outcome of a 1977 fire was the hand-stencilled ceiling, designed by the architect Gerald Robinson, a member of the parish.

This is one of the few religious institutions in Toronto that continues to have the same kind of vibrant connection with its community as churches in Europe, in the centre of urban activity, furnishing as well a pleasant space to relax in. The City had the good sense in 1985 to retain the architect Ron Thom and the landscape architect Stephen Moorhouse to create on the south side of the church an urban park with paved areas and a lawn, as well as to re-create the course of a forgotten stream that flows along the walkway through to Bay Street. The Marriott Hotel to the northwest has taken advantage of this scene by locating its coffee shop to overlook Trinity Square.

Inside Holy Trinity in 1913.

COMMERCE COURT NORTH

25 King Street West (at Jordan Street)

T he original Bank of Commerce building (as it was called from 1931, when it opened, until the mid-1970s) contains one of the city's most spectacular banking halls—a sixty-five-foot-high vaulted ceiling with octagonal coffers painted in buff and blue with gilt mouldings over a floor of Italian travertine marble.

Shown here just after completion in 1930, the Bank of Commerce building remained the tallest in the Commonwealth until 1962 (CTA 1244-3181).

The azure blue in the ceiling was apparently chosen after a diligent search by the architect John Pearson, who finally discovered the exact desired shade on the back of a construction worker—he purchased the shirt for $2 and the master painter used it as his reference.

On the south wall of the banking hall is a memorial screen to bank employees who died in the Great War. It was designed by the Canadian sculptor Emanuel Hahn and executed in situ by John Donnelly of New York and William Dawson of Montreal.

The main banking hall, modelled after the Baths of Caracella in Rome, boasts three bronze chandeliers and walls faced with limestone from Virginia.

Such splendid elements must surely have made customers feel confident in the institution's substance and reliability. Leading from either side of the banking hall are smaller vaulted spaces lined with marvellous oil paintings by Arthur Crisp, a native of Hamilton, Ontario, depicting scenes from the history of Canadian transportation. While (sadly) the hall has been broken into smaller offices for private banking and some sections are closed to public access, the space is still impressive.

The exterior, clad in Indiana limestone, has a monumental presence. It was designed in the late 1920s by the New York firm of bank architects York and Sawyer, working with Toronto partners Darling & Pearson, and for many decades it was the tallest structure (thirty-four storeys) in the Commonwealth. Barely visible from the street, near the top of the structure, are giant heads—four on each side of the building—passively gazing across the changing city, with beards flowing ten feet down the walls. They are positioned around what in the past was a viewing platform, now closed to the public.

The grand entrance on King Street clearly signals visitors to be both impressed and made welcome. The arched surround is covered with carvings of bees, squirrels, and other animals symbolizing thrift and industry, and in the semi-circular panel above the doors are female figures of

One of the "Sixteen Giants of Jordan Street" casts its gaze across Toronto, circa 1930. Two designs—one serious, one smiling—alternate around the tower, marking the level of the former viewing platform, sadly now off-limits to the public, due to safety regulations.

Industry and Commerce, as well as a grain elevator, flying geese, and the outline of this building itself. Animal motifs are continued inside the building: small owls perch on the brass door frames, and birds and squirrels are carved in the soft honey-coloured stone of the elevator foyer.

The Commerce Court complex followed the merger of the Imperial Bank of Canada and the Bank of Commerce in the late 1960s. Like the marriage of the Toronto and Dominion Banks a few years earlier (its progeny is the TD Centre across the street), this union resulted in a new large office project.

Commerce Court West, designed by I. M. Pei and the Toronto firm Page and Steele in the early 1970s, is a box of glass and stainless steel rising relentlessly fifty-seven storeys, an example of the International Style. The front door of the Bank of Commerce may be welcoming and audacious, but Commerce Court West makes no such grand and inviting gesture. The entryway is difficult to identify, merely a revolving glass door in a glass wall, and even that is lodged under a wide and apparently weight-bearing beam just eight feet above the ground. Perhaps responding to the slightly unsettling quality of this element, pedestrians appear to scurry inside to safety. The building is without exterior detail, and there is no awe-inspiring banking hall inside; instead, the main interior design feature seems to be an escalator slowly descending to a concourse level.

Recent attempts to soften the Commerce Court complex include additions by Toronto's Zeidler Roberts Partnership in the 1990s: a rugged metal link between the old Bank and the new tower, and in the courtyard jagged windows rising like pointed scallops on a dragon's back from the underground concourse.

COURTHOUSE MARKET GRILLE AND CHAMBER LOUNGE

57 Adelaide Street East

The York County Court House was built in the heart of the booming city in the mid-nineteenth century to serve two purposes—as a home for York County Council and as a new courthouse.

The main entrance to the Courthouse Market Grille, formerly the York County Court House.

The building was designed in 1851 by Frederic W. Cumberland (of the firm Cumberland & Ridout), architect for other important Toronto structures such as St. James' Cathedral, University College, the Chapel of St. James-the-Less, and the central portion of Osgoode Hall. The four plain, strong pillars are surmounted by a heavy entablature, making the front "austere, heavy and forbidding" (according to Eric Arthur), but in today's environment it clearly adds formal solidity to an otherwise disheartening stretch of nondescript buildings on this block.

The main entrance way, now to the left, was originally between the two central pillars, leading through the lobby (now the front dining room) to the court—used as recently as the 1960s for that purpose—now the main dining room, with a fine stone fireplace. On the second floor was the York County Council Chamber, accessed by the staircase just beyond the lobby. The Chamber is a magnificent space, a large cube pierced by a heavy chandelier. Currently it serves as a dance club on weekends, with patrons having a good view of activities from the balcony. Offices for the court and county were found on either side, as well as on the third floor. The wings on either side of the building have since been demolished. In the basement, near the washrooms, is a restored jail cell occupied by a long-term and ultimately harmless wax figure, staring out from behind the bars. The adjacent cell can be rented for more intimate dinner parties.

> The Arts and Letters Club established its first offices in the courthouse in 1909 and stayed for a decade. The Club inspired many artistic events, including performances by the cellist Pablo Casals and the Russian pianist and composer Sergei Rachmaninov, and laid the foundations for the Toronto Symphony Orchestra and the Mendelssohn Choir.

The rear facade has none of the grandeur of the Adelaide Street frontage: its brick and carefully placed windows give it the air of a Georgian residential block. To the south is a space that was empty until quite recently. At one time another courthouse stood just off King Street, with a jail beside it, at the corner of King and Toronto Streets. Once the jail was closed in 1838, the space at its rear remained vacant. In the 1990s, the area finally received attention from the City—financing and design professionals were provided, and Courthouse Square, as it is now called, consists of plantings, a water course, seating, and mysterious objects with obscure post-modern sayings carved into them.

At least one bench sits on large marble law books. This pleasant park could very well note, but doesn't, that two leaders of the failed Rebellion of 1837, Peter Matthews and Samuel Lount, were executed by hanging on a scaffold erected here in 1838. (The men are now buried in the Necropolis, on Winchester Street, in Cabbagetown, with a memorial there honouring their lives.) Outdoor tables for the Courthouse Market Grille spill out onto the square, to the delight of its patrons, but the occasional complaints of residents of the new apartments to the immediate south mark the age-old, usually resolvable, dispute between different users of urban space.

In its prime, other important structures were gathered around the courthouse. To the west, the former Trust and Loan building still stands, a simple but elegant example of the Renaissance Revival style, now home to a restaurant. Around the corner on Toronto Street are the Seventh Post Office and the former Consumers Gas building, now the Rosewater Supper Club.

The front dining room.

Diagonally across Adelaide Street from the courthouse once stood the Eighth Post Office. This was an astonishing Second Empire building, with columns, large arched windows, cornices, keystones, a pediment, and a high vaulted roof, that would have looked right at home in Paris. However, in 1957 it was deemed inappropriate for the modern city, and in 1960 it was demolished to make way for a federal office building. This new structure was something of a gamble for the federal government: as the Toronto subway was being constructed down Yonge Street in the early 1950s, much thought was given as to whether Toronto's business district would expand to the east or the west from its centre at King and Yonge Streets. The federal government put its money on the eastern option and purchased this site. It commissioned the largest office building the city had ever seen, over half a million square feet, in the International Style, with a courtyard at grade. As luck would have it, the downtown then expanded in the opposite direction, as the subway turned west from Union Station and headed north under University Avenue, leaving the federal building out of the main action. The name of the city's first mayor, William Lyon Mackenzie, was stuck on the structure—hardly a compliment to his style and vision. The building became redundant within a few decades but has now received a fine new silver skin and full interior rehabilitation to serve its restored life as an office building. Behind it, on the Lombard Street side, the stone carving of the royal arms that once crowned the front door of the Eighth Post Office sits marooned on the ground.

Looking north along Toronto Street in 1907 to the Eighth Post Office (demolished in 1960) on Adelaide Street (CTA SC231-1668).

DESIGN EXCHANGE

234 Bay Street

The entrance to the Design Exchange.

The Design Exchange began life as the Toronto Stock Exchange in 1937. A wonderful example of Art Deco style in structure and detail, it was designed by George and Moorehouse.

Across the granite and limestone facade runs a bas-relief frieze of Canadian workers. (It's hard to find stone friezes in Toronto: the only other example that comes to mind is on the exterior of the Royal Ontario Museum.) Various kinds of workers march by in this design by Charles Comfort, executed by Peter Schoem. Four figures from the right, wearing a top hat, is a businessman with his hand apparently in the pocket of the worker in front of him.

This facade, with five tall windows above the frieze, doors and smaller windows below, is somewhat constrained by the office tower that since 1994 has surrounded and surmounted it. The new structure is not of the purity of the adjacent Ludwig Mies van der Rohe structures but contains strange angled details that unsuccessfully try to bridge the two architectural styles.

The current management of the Design Exchange is unhappy with the street presence of the building, and, in the face of strong opposition from the city's heritage community, has obtained City Council's approval to create a large picture window between the two sets of doors, in the expectation that this will make the interior more inviting. The intermediate compromise to street visibility seems to be the forest of light standards on the sidewalk, illuminating the exterior in the evening hours.

Inside, the ground floor is generally open to the public, with an exhibition area for Canadian design and a bar and restaurant. On the

The former trading floor of the TSE, with four of Charles Comfort's murals in the background.

next level up is the former trading floor of the Toronto Stock Exchange, two storeys high, showing much Art Deco detail, including eight large paintings by Charles Comfort, which, like the frieze, celebrate Canadian industry. The room has a fine delicate quality of light, although it undoubtedly misses the hectic activity that reigned until the Stock Exchange moved one block west in the 1980s and then vanished altogether into electronic space.

As new user of the space, the Design Exchange itself is a very interesting idea. It was formed in the early 1990s to showcase and collect examples of Canadian design, on the assumption that design always adds more value than cost. When originally conceived, the Design Exchange saw its role as a public institution, encouraging people to attend exhibits, discussions, and presentations. Recently it has become more private in nature, catering to the events of companies able to pay their own way.

Customers at the Toronto Stock Exchange watch the trading board, circa 1920 (CTA 1244-144).

DU TOIT ALLSOPP HILLIER

50 Park Road

One of the most pleasing International Style buildings in Toronto is at **50 Park Road.** It resulted from a design competition held by the Ontario Association of Architects for its offices, won by John B. Parkin Associates, later a very influential firm in Toronto. (Their equally impressive Ortho Pharmaceutical plant on Greenbelt Drive in Don Mills—a fine example of Modernist architecture—was designed several years after this structure.

The building, opened in 1954, is simplicity itself. The south and west walls are yellow brick; the east wall is glass and yellow brick; and the north wall is glass and steel. The proportions of the structure and its elements are clean and precise. Every dimension is a multiple of a five-foot module; the building is forty feet wide, eighty feet deep, and twenty feet high.

The interior is also clean and simple, with an expansive main foyer and a large work space on the north side of the building, in spite of the small size of the structure. The Parkin firm designed all items in the building—lighting fixtures, tableware, furniture—and sought out Canadian manufacturers. Harold Kalman notes in *A History of Canadian Architecture* that "in order to raise money for the new pieces, the Association sold the antique furniture from its previous headquarters . . . dispensing with traditional design literally as well as symbolically." Originally a ramp linked the two floors, but it has been replaced by a stairway. The lower level served as a dining room, which became a prominent part in the social life of Toronto architects and proved to create cohesiveness and collegiality in the profession: they would bring clients here for lunch to discuss their latest projects and ideas. The lower level has been divided into offices. Even with these changes, this remains a very satisfying building, inside and out.

By the early 1990s the Ontario Association of Architects moved to a larger space, and the building was purchased by the current occupants, du Toit Allsopp Hillier, urban designers and architects with a long list of notable projects and design awards to their name, including the plan for the parliamentary precinct and Confederation Boulevard in Ottawa, campus plans for many Canadian universities, and a heritage plan for the Gooderham and Worts complex.

The area around the building has a fascinating history. Park Road was the first entry point to the Rosedale subdivision that William Jarvis embarked on in 1852. (He and his wife had lived in a house near what is now 9 Cluny Drive before the subdivision was proposed.) The challenge was crossing the creek that ran in a course now followed by Rosedale Valley Road—Park Road was the chosen route. The subdivision floundered in an economic recession until Jarvis's nephew built a house in 1866 at the northeast corner of Park Road and the creek. (It still survives as part of Branksome Hall.) The bridge over the creek collapsed in 1872, killing a delivery man, and has since been enclosed in a sewer pipe. Rosedale has thrived for more than a century.

To the west of 50 Park Road, at the end of the short cul-de-sac across the lawn, is the Studio Building, used in the early decades of the twentieth century by Tom Thomson and his painter friends who, three years after his death in 1917, would form the Group of Seven.

ELGIN AND WINTER GARDEN THEATRE CENTRE

189 Yonge Street

The Elgin and Winter Garden Theatre Centre is the only double-decker complex in the world continuing to serve its original function. It was designed by the prominent New York architect Thomas Lamb just before the First World War to provide a venue for both vaudeville and silent films.

Its entrance on Yonge Street is lavish and inviting, with finely decorated doors and a generous marquee under three large arched windows. Like many other theatre complexes that did not wish to occupy the most expensive land, it has only the entrance on the main street: a walkway leads straight from Yonge Street for fifty yards to the theatres on Victoria Street, to the rear.

This concourse is very showy. Wall-to-wall mirrors trimmed with gold leaf and twinkling chandeliers ensure that going to the theatre is a way of displaying oneself while gawking at others doing the same.

The concourse leads to the Elgin Theatre, originally built by Marcus Loew as a jewel in his chain of Canadian vaudeville theatres. The theatre has three boxes on either side of the stage, decorated in a golden brocade and ironwork, including the outline of jester heads. The walls are covered with a red-and-gold fabric, and the large proscenium arch stage has a golden crest over it. The ceiling is high, with ornate plaster moulding and gilt-painted detail. The room has been restored as a most elegant space for live theatre, with excellent acoustics.

In the foyer area, elevator and escalator lift patrons over the roof of the Elgin up to the Winter Garden Theatre. (Be warned, the wide flowing staircase offers a long climb.) Opened in 1914, several months after the Elgin, the Winter Garden is atmospheric and unusual. Suspended from the ceiling are bunches of leaves, conveying a sense of the outdoors—theatre under the protection of trees. There's even a painted moon at the left of the stage, whose curtain is appropriately decorated with a sylvan scene.

The world changed quickly for these two promising venues after they opened. By the early 1930s talking pictures were the rage, and vaudeville had declined in popularity. The Winter Garden had already closed in 1928; the Elgin was wired for sound and became Loew's Downtown, a movie theatre, until the early '80s. The Winter Garden remained unknown by most Torontonians for almost fifty years.

During the 1970s the theatre community established a real presence in Toronto, and the opportunity was seen to renovate the two theatres and again use them as self-sustaining performance spaces. In 1981 the Ontario Heritage Foundation purchased the complex and restored it to its former glory at a cost of $29 million. Some of this money was raised by the sale of unneeded density rights to a developer on Wellington Street, permitting an office building between Bay and York to be several storeys higher than otherwise allowed.

The Elgin Theatre, after restoration by the Ontario Heritage Foundation.

The Winter Garden Theatre, reopened to the public after being unused for fifty years.

Restoration was carried out under the direction of the architect Mandel Sprachman, who had successfully tackled other theatre conversions, including, in the 1970s, the Pantages (now the Canon). Extraordinary work was carried out: hundreds of pounds of bread dough, for example, were used to clean the handpainted watercolour walls of the Winter Garden. Some five thousand branches of beech leaves were harvested and fireproofed, to be suspended from the ceiling. Many thousands of wafer-thin sheets of aluminum leaf were needed to rebuild the plaster details in the Elgin, and the ersatz marble veining in the lobby and grand staircase required much attention. In the lobby of the structure (now called the Thomas Lamb Lobby), no less than twenty-eight layers of paint were removed to reveal the original surface. Great pains were taken to preserve the integrity of the original features, including the decision not to correct the misspelling of a composer's name uncovered in the main concourse.

In 1985 the Elgin was reopened, followed four years later by the Winter Garden. Crush space was added to the front of the building, as well as new escalators, and to the rear, dressing rooms and loading docks were improved.

Although tours are offered regularly, the best way to experience these theatres is to attend a performance.

FAIRMONT ROYAL YORK HOTEL

100 Front Street West

The lobby.

This is the grande dame of Toronto hotels. It was designed by Ross and Macdonald in the late 1920s (at the same time the firm was designing Eaton's College Street), and they created a building as substantial as railway travellers might expect, with the added benefit of a roofline like a château. Set across the street from the city's main railway station, it was one in the Canadian Pacific Railway's successful creation of a string of superior railway hotels across Canada.

The structure is dressed in restrained grey stone enlivened by decorative carved squares. The first three storeys are set apart from the rest of the building by a band of decorated stone. As a further way to reduce the bulk of the structure, the central portion is set back from the fifth floor up, so that the ends of the building become wings. The recessed central structure rises and steps back in a tiered fashion, repeats the design elements of columns and arches that are over the main entrance, reaching a final crescendo in a decorated parapet some twenty-six storeys high, over which is a steeply pitched copper roof pierced by gables, finished with a rising chimney. All in all it is a solid, massive building, boasting in its heyday 1,048 rooms and a telephone switchboard with

Hotel switchboard workers.

thirty-five operators. The Front and York Street facades include, as a serious design element, many shallow balconies—one can imagine royalty leaning out and waving.

Through the main doors a half-dozen steps lead to the large and comfortable lobby, two storeys high, surrounded by a mezzanine and filled with stuffed furniture and rugs laid over a mosaic floor. At the west end of the lobby is the Imperial Room, at one time the most chic supper club in Toronto, tastefully designed on two levels with a small stage, a coffered ceiling, and windows with heavy draperies. Leading from other parts of the lobby are lounges and restaurants. It is clearly a stately and opulent place to welcome guests to the city.

This hotel has splendid rooms for meetings and conferences, and since the service provided is excellent, it is heavily booked. On the mezzanine level, meeting rooms are decorated to reflect the character of each province. The British Columbia Room has a painting of mountains looming over a stormy sound;

Steam engines at the eastern entrance to Union Station, circa 1930, with the Royal York Hotel in the background.

the Saskatchewan Room shows vast wheat fields; the Manitoba Room features buffalo on the prairies.

Above the mezzanine, on the second floor, the public rooms are more appropriate for larger gatherings. The most spectacular is the Ballroom, the windows of which look onto Front Street from above the main entrance. This space is commodious, two storeys high and decorated in an eclectic manner. On the ceiling is a large painting of a woman (perhaps Diana, Goddess of the Hunt) in a chariot being pulled by two large and reluctant bulls. Other Greek motifs are incorporated in the decoration, and the cut-glass chandeliers add a festive note. When the ballroom is crowded with people, it is difficult to picture a more celebratory space anywhere in the city. At the west end of the floor, the Concert Hall is restrained and beautiful with its large chandelier, arched windows, and colourful rug. At the east end, the Canadian Room is sedate, its carved wood showing the Canadian coat of arms and provincial crests.

When first built, this was one of the largest hotels in the Commonwealth, and it still remains a key place for the business community in Toronto to meet and to lodge its guests.

The Ballroom.

FLATIRON (GOODERHAM) BUILDING

49 Wellington Street East

A view of the Flatiron Building, looking west.

Georg Gooderham was one of Toronto's leading businessmen in the latter part of the nineteenth century. His father had been a founder of the very successful Gooderham and Worts distillery, and George increased his inherited wealth in other successful ventures, including Manufacturers' Life and the Bank of Toronto.

Gooderham was one of the richest men in the city. He lived in a large Victorian pile on the northeast corner of Bloor and St. George Streets, now occupied by the York Club. He wanted an office building and purchased the thin wedge-shaped parcel of land at Wellington and Church Streets, then known as the Coffin Block because of the chunky

Visitors exploring the building at Doors Open 2001.

shape of the structure occupying it. In 1892 he hired the local architect David Roberts Jr., designer of many buildings in the Gooderham and Worts complex, as well as the Gooderham home.

Roberts placed Gooderham's office right in the narrow wedge of the building with marvellous rounded windows overlooking the family's distillery to the east, the market and city hall immediately below on the street, and the railway and port to the south. North across Wellington Street was Gooderham's Bank of Toronto building (since demolished), so naturally a tunnel was constructed under the road to link the two buildings. Gooderham was said to have liked "fresh money," and he exchanged his soiled bills at his bank for cleaner ones.

The building is dressed in red brick and red Credit Valley sandstone. Its narrow height is emphasized by the brick piers that run three storeys up between generous windows before being broken by a small cornice, then continue two storeys to end in arched windows, a more elaborate cornice, and a steeply pitched copper roof with dormer windows. This feeling of height is even further augmented by the peaked tower at the eastern end of the building. The main door on the north side is covered by a large broad arch and intricate stone carving. Inside is a lobby with a handsome staircase and a small elevator in a wrought-iron cage—the

One of the rich details of the building's Richardson Romanesque-style carving.

first electric elevator in the city and one of the few that continue to be manually operated. Most rooms seem overwhelmed by the light from the large windows, which are handsomely sashed and open to permit an exchange of city air.

The park immediately to the west of the Flatiron is named after William Berczy. He was born in Germany in 1744, trained in Vienna, worked in England, immigrated to New York in 1792, and came to Upper Canada in 1794, two years later than John Graves Simcoe. He was an architect and painter and earned his living exclusively from portraits and other painting from 1805 until his death in 1813. He painted the famous portrait of Joseph Brant, the Mohawk chief who sided with the British in the Seven Years War, which resulted in the British defeat of Montcalm at Quebec in 1759. Brant later established what became known as the Six Nations Reserve on the Grand River near Brantford.

The buildings on the block to the west have been demolished, and a trompe l'oeil mural by Derek Besant has been affixed to the butt end of this structure, overlooking a small park. The mural shows a curtain about to be drawn, reflecting the late 1970s, when this area was touted as Toronto's theatre district, given the nearby existence of the St. Lawrence Centre and the O'Keefe (Hummingbird) Centre, although history has not borne that promise out. The 1980 mural has two compelling aspects: it pretends that many windows pierce this end of the building when in fact only one does; second, the design of the painted red brick piers in the mural is taken from the building at 41–43 Front Street East, a fine warehouse constructed in the 1860s and now renovated into office space. The Flatiron Building is such an attractive counterpoint to the large ungainly towers to the west that it is one of the most photographed structures in Toronto.

HELICONIAN HALL

35 Hazelton Avenue

Inside Heliconian Hall.

When Olivet Church, now at 35 Hazelton Avenue, was built in 1875, Yorkville was still a village; another few years would pass before it was amalgamated into the City of Toronto.

The building is made of wood (board and batten is the style) with none of the stone and brick sophistication of other churches in the growing city, but the detail is very fine. In deference to wood's characteristics, sharp curves have been avoided: the Gothic arch over each door is considerably softened, and the window arches have become simple triangles. The structure was originally built at the corner of Scollard but was moved slightly north in 1890 to make way for the new and larger Olivet Church in Victorian red sandstone and brick, now standing at the corner and converted to galleries and offices. The wooden building became the church hall and Sunday school.

Inside the building is a single room, with a vaulted ceiling laced with beams. The rose window, a focus of the building's facade, serves the same function for the rear wall inside, providing handsome illumination as well. There is a large brick fireplace on the south wall, and a stage at the east end, behind which is the kitchen and a reception room. The hall seats about a hundred, and acoustics for the concerts and other cultural events held here are excellent.

The Toronto Heliconian Club was founded in 1893 by Mary Hewitt Smart, a singing teacher at the Toronto Conservatory of Music. It provided a comfortable venue for women interested in culture and the arts. The name was suggested by Goldwin Smith, Sage of the Grange, after Mount Helena, home of the muses. The Club moved here in 1923, using it as a place for exhibits, lectures, discussions, and social events. Many authors have spoken here—Mazo de la Roche, E. J. Pratt, and Ralph Connor are a few—and many artists have shown their works. As women have been permitted to join other organizations in the city, the Heliconian Club has expanded its activities, making this space available for use by others.

In the 1960s this area, Yorkville, was the centre of hippie culture in Toronto, with coffeehouses and clubs featuring young singers such as Gordon Lightfoot and Joni Mitchell. Yorkville has since moved considerably upscale although its contemporary architecture tends to be undistinguished compared with the houses of Hazelton Avenue.

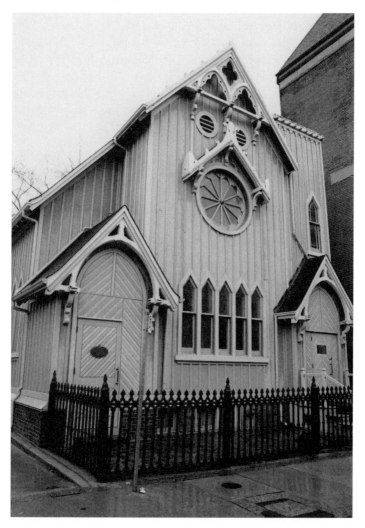

HUMMINGBIRD CENTRE FOR THE PERFORMING ARTS

1 Front Street East

The flat clear surfaces of the exterior, the lack of colour and decoration, and the clean lines of the structure are a good example of the 1950s Modernist skills of the influential and prolific English-born architect **Peter Dickinson.** He also designed the Benvenuto Place apartments on Avenue Road (replacing the eponymous nineteenth-century mansion) and the strange brick apartment towers in Regent Park South.

There are few buildings in Toronto that are as elegant and appealing in expressing the Modern style as this theatre. The huge cantilevered canopy over the main doors and its bright lighting give theatregoers an immediate sense of the drama and importance of events here.

This theatre, opened in 1960, was built by the financier E. P. Taylor's O'Keefe Brewery after he had been cajoled by Mayor Nathan Phillips in 1954 to do something for the arts in Toronto. It is still known to many Torontonians as the O'Keefe Centre. After several decades, the company tired of paying the operating deficits; Metro Toronto took it over and found a way to make it break even. In 1996 Hummingbird

The lobby, showing York Wilson's mural, *The Seven Lively Arts.*

The first show to open was a pre-Broadway showing of the Lerner and Loewe musical *Camelot*, starring Richard Burton, Julie Andrews, and Robert Goulet.

Communications, a Toronto software company, renamed it after making a $5 million donation for building improvements.

Inside the front doors one is immediately struck by the generous foyer, and the large mural by York Wilson, *The Seven Lively Arts*, each of which can be identified. The theatre space itself is considered by many to be somewhat too large (seating thirty-two hundred people) and the acoustics, although much improved over the years (special wood panelling on the walls, for instance), still leave something to be desired.

The building is used regularly by the Canadian Opera Company and the National Ballet of Canada, both of whom wish to build their own facilities but remain here because of the excellent backstage facilities. The amalgamation of Toronto in 1998 has led many city councillors to suggest the structure be sold (and demolished), but it seems that decision will not be made until the opera and ballet have new quarters for themselves. This fine example of period architecture should not be lost.

The Hummingbird (then the O'Keefe) Centre hosted perhaps the most important event in national culture, the Canadian Conference of the Arts in May 1961. The speakers' list is a who's who from the mid-twentieth century: Northrop Frye, Leonard Cohen, Earle Birney, the University of Toronto president Claude Bissell, the theatre philanthropist Arthur Gelber, the visual artists Harold Town and Alex Colville, and the writers Mordecai Richler, Hugh MacLennan, and Morley Callaghan, among others. Greg Gatenby writes in Toronto: A Literary Guide that the conference "served the purpose of having the arts—and the problems of the artists in Toronto—taken seriously by the media and by politicians."

ISABEL BADER THEATRE

📋 93 Charles Street West

The north entrance.

This building is an act of love. Alfred Bader and Isabel Overton were Canadian students who met while vacationing in England in the late 1940s. They fell in love, but as he was Jewish and she Christian, she decided it was best if they went their separate ways. Twenty-five years later, they met again and married.

Isabel, a graduate of Victoria College, spent many years teaching drama in England. When Alfred approached the college in the late 1990s to donate a gift in his wife's name, he proposed buying the Old Vic in London, England, for the "new" Vic in Toronto. But the president of Victoria College brought him around to the felicitous idea of commemorating his wife and her interest in drama by building this theatre.

The building sits comfortably between Burwash Hall on the east and Emmanuel College to the west, following the same streetline and rooflines as those buildings and using the same limestone cladding. The glass and doors on the Charles Street frontage soften the transition between the inside and the outside of the building, and the ochre slate tiles beside the main entrance provide a slight hint of warmth. Inside, the lobby is small but pleasant with exposed concrete columns, a marble floor, and much glass, permitting views into the interior of the block. The theatre itself is intimate, accommodating five hundred people in seating around the perimeter of the auditorium, creating a continuity between those on the stage and those in the audience. The colours are subdued greys and purples, with Jatoba wood as an accent, making the space appropriate as a classroom for lectures during the school day and performances at other times. Latticework on the side walls helps diffuse the sound, and a reflector above the balcony is said to improve the clarity of music at the rear of the theatre. To ensure that the height of the building is comparable with that of its neighbours, a floor has been added, occupied by the Department of Comparative Literature.

This theatre, which opened in March 2001, was designed by Peter Smith of the Toronto firm Lett/Smith Architects, also responsible for the Princess of Wales Theatre on King Street West and the du Maurier Theatre at Harbourfront.

The lobby with Victoria College's main building visible through the window.

MACKENZIE HOUSE

82 Bond Street

William Lyon Mackenzie is a large figure in Toronto's, and indeed Canada's, history. He came to the Town of York in 1820 from Scotland at the age of twenty-five, opening a retail shop with his friend John Lesslie on the south side of King Street, across from St. James' Church.

Within four years, he began publishing the *Colonial Advocate*, a newspaper that defined progressive politics in Upper Canada, creating both an agenda for change and a language for the public about the Family Compact (as he called them) which ruled Upper Canada. Mackenzie rejected the idea that a small group of self-appointed people (which is how he saw the Family Compact) should make decisions with wide public impact. Four years later, in 1828, he was elected to the Legislative Assembly, where his brilliant strategies upset and infuriated the Family Compact. Mackenzie created a large constituency for change based on self-rule and attention to social justice. He faced a stormy time in the Legislature and was thrown out on many occasions when government leaders did not like what he was saying. On every occasion he was re-elected to the same position, often by acclamation. When the Town of York was reorganized to become the City of Toronto in 1834, Mackenzie was elected its first mayor, to the horror of the Family Compact. He served well, although the challenges of establishing and then operating a municipal structure were immense, and the city was thrust into the midst of a cholera epidemic. He decided not to seek re-election as mayor, and after one year again turned his energies to the Legislature of Upper Canada.

In 1836 Sir Francis Bond Head, the lieutenant-governor, used public funds to influence voters and instigated violence in the election to such an extent that Mackenzie and most other reformers were not re-elected. For the next eighteen months, debates raged over future strategy, with Mackenzie playing a lead role. With the beginning of open rebellion in Lower Canada in the fall of 1837, Mackenzie and other reformers decided on the same course of action in Upper Canada. The Rebellion of 1837 lasted no more than a week and was unsuccessful. While Mackenzie was sheltered by his many friends and supporters, who helped him escape across the American border at Niagara Falls, a number of leading rebels were captured and executed. Mackenzie stayed in exile in the United States until 1850, and on his return to Upper Canada he was immediately elected to the Legislature. Some of the changes he had pushed for—such as more local autonomy (responsible government)—had been accomplished, but exile had broken him. His voice seemed more shrill, and he no longer had the

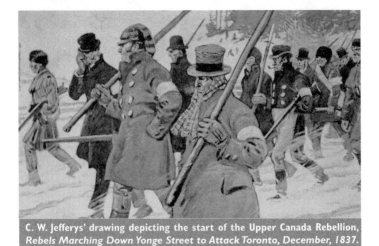

C. W. Jefferys' drawing depicting the start of the Upper Canada Rebellion, *Rebels Marching Down Yonge Street to Attack Toronto, December, 1837.*

important friendship or the same critical political knowledge. Yet he was a hero to many people in spite of what appeared to be eccentricities.

James Lesslie, a former member of Toronto City Council in 1834 and a successful businessman (and brother of John Lesslie) undertook a public subscription in the 1850s to honour Mackenzie and provide his family with a home. Mackenzie and his large family had hovered on the brink of poverty because his publishing activities—he continued to publish newspapers in the U.S. as well as during the years after his return to Upper Canada—often operated at a loss. A substantial sum of almost $8,000 was collected, and this property at 82 Bond Street was purchased. Mackenzie and his family moved into the house in 1858, and he died here in 1861. His wife and daughters remained for several decades.

The house is plain in style with none of the elegant Georgian details of a home of a more well-to-do family. Entry to the building is now by a sidewalk leading to the rear, where there is a walled garden and bas-relief sculptures by Emanuel Hahn (after drawings by C. W. Jefferys) of Mackenzie and his colleagues Samuel Lount and Peter Matthews, both of whom were hanged after the Rebellion. The Toronto historian William Dendy noted that these were originally commissioned by the Niagara Parks Commission but stored away and neglected until they were rediscovered and donated to the city in the 1970s. (There is a small arch at the corner of Yonge and McGill Streets—one street north of Gerrard Street—containing other portions of the same memorial.)

A printing press has been established at the rear of the property, giving the flavour of Mackenzie's famous print shop on Frederick Street, which was broken into in 1826 by young members of the Family Compact who stole the type and tossed it into Toronto Bay. One can purchase duplicate copies of the *Colonial Advocate*, and the gift shop has interesting material about the Rebellion and Mackenzie's role in it.

The house is maintained to provide a good idea of the kinds of colour, wall coverings, and furniture in Toronto interiors in the 1860s. There are rumours of the ghost of a grey lady on the second floor, but no one has seen her of late.

J. W. L. Forster's portrait of William Lyon Mackenzie (1795–1861), journalist, politician, and a key figure in creating accountable government in Canada.

Mackenzie's most powerful statement for parliamentary reform in Upper Canada is found in the Seventh Report of the Grievances Committee, a committee of the Legislature that he chaired in 1835. The following is a brief excerpt from the report, which he probably wrote himself:

"The affairs of this country have been ever against the spirit of the constitutional act, subjected in the most injurious manner to the interferences and interdictions of a succession of Colonial ministers in England who have never visited the country, and can never possibly become acquainted with the state of parties, or the conduct of public functionaries, except through official channels... which are illy calculated to convey the information necessary to... correct public abuses.
A painful experience has proved how impracticable it is for such a succession of strangers beneficially to direct and control the affairs of the people 4000 miles off; and being an impracticable system, felt to be intolerable by those for whose good it was professedly intended, it ought to be abolished, and the domestic institutions of the province so improved and administered by the local authorities...."

MARKET GALLERY

95 Front Street East

The Front Street City Hall was built on the site of the Home District Farmers' Storehouse. This photo was taken in 1899, the same year that a larger City Hall was completed at 60 Queen Street West (CTA SC231-98).

York's Town Hall was located on King Street near Jarvis, and was used primarily for social events until the creation of the City of Toronto in 1834. From then on it functioned as the City Hall until Council undertook this new building on Front Street in the mid-1840s. It remained in use until the third City Hall—now known as Old City Hall—was completed in 1899.

The Front Street City Hall was designed by Henry Bowyer Lane, architect of the Church of the Holy Trinity and Little Trinity Church. The wings of the building have been demolished, as have the pediment and the tower. The central section remains, with a major addition to the south, new wings, and a new roofline.

City Council met on the second floor of the central portion of this building. The mayor's chair can still be found, but the space has been entirely renovated for use as the city's gallery for displays of items relating to civic history. A police station occupied space on the first floor, and in the basement were cells, frequently flooded by water from the bay that lapped at the building's walls. Today, this part of the building is often just a passageway for customers of the two floors of food shops under the expansive vault over the main part of the building. The existence of this whole structure is the result of a significant political battle more than three decades ago.

In 1970 City Council decided that the building on the site, then in poor structural condition, should be demolished and replaced by a parking garage. Considerable citizen opposition forced the abandonment of the proposal and a decision to rebuild the market and rehabilitate the municipal building. That led to even more remarkable change: with these signs of regeneration, the reform Council elected in 1972 decided to undertake the development of the St. Lawrence community in the immediate vicinity. At forty-five acres, this was the largest renewal project in a North American city centre during the twentieth century. In March 1979 the Market Gallery of the City of Toronto Archives opened as a place to house and display Toronto's art and archival collections, as well as exhibits about the city's past.

Outside, an interesting perspective on the St. Lawrence community is gained from the south deck of the market building, which is twenty feet above the street. Originally this deck extended over water (the gentle slope of the road at Front Street was the edge of the bay), but landfill has reached past the Esplanade, where the railways originally seized city parkland for their own use, south past the railway embankment and the Gardiner Expressway, as far as the Redpath Sugar plant, whose chunky form is just visible from the south deck.

The area on the north side of Front Street has served continuously as a farmers' market from the earliest founding days of the Town of York. Saturday is market day, but the current structure,

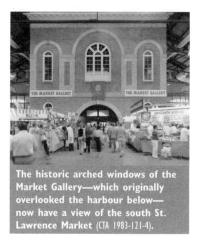

The historic arched windows of the Market Gallery—which originally overlooked the harbour below— now have a view of the south St. Lawrence Market (CTA 1983-121-4).

Toronto City Hall, Council Chamber, 1899 showing a meeting in session (CTA SC246-49).

Standing in front of the Market Gallery affords a fine view east along Front Street of the evolving city. The city's weigh scales once stood at the northeast corner of Front and Jarvis (appropriately close to the market, since farmers were the scales' main users), now marked by a small monument. Not all the buildings on the north side of Front running east from Jarvis are original: a close look will show that in the past twenty years several have been designed and built to fit in very attractively with those first constructed about 1840. The bell tower of St. Lawrence Hall can be seen hovering above the Farmers' Market, and to the west, Market Street has been closed to create a pedestrian mall. Next to it is the Market Square condominium, where the architect Jerome Markson has designed housing in a contemporary style that harmonizes with the older structures in the area.

designed by the architectural historian Eric Arthur, is often criticized as lacking any expression of the vitality of the market. For many decades in the twentieth century, a roof extended over Front Street, linking the Farmers' Market to the south building. This was demolished in 1954, when it was declared unsafe.

MASSEY HALL

178 Victoria Street (at Shuter Street)

Whent Massey Hall opened in 1894, *Canadian Architect and Builder* said that its exterior was "about as aesthetical as the average grain elevator." Certainly the dirty patina of city dust and the iron fire escapes drooping awkwardly toward the street have done nothing to enhance its appearance over time. The underlying design is quite simple: the facade divided into three parts, each with three sets of windows with intervening fluted pilasters, and a pediment over the middle section.

Inside Massey Hall, 1894.

The hall, designed by S. R. Badgley of Cleveland, was built for Canada's leading industrialist, Hart Massey, as a memorial to his eldest son, Charles, who had died of typhoid in 1884. It was the first dedicated music and concert hall (apart from the city's theatres) that could accommodate a large group of musicians. Greg Gatenby notes in *Toronto: A Literary Guide* that "no proper Methodist would be caught dead entering such a wicked, sinful hovel as a theatre, no matter how pure the music on stage." And so, to distinguish this space from a theatre, there is no proscenium arch: the stage spills right out to the audience. Apparently Hart Massey boasted that he had never entered a theatre in his whole life.

When the building was constructed, the Masseys were told that the copper nails holding the slate roof tiles in place would last a hundred years. Indeed they did, but no longer—they were replaced in the early 1990s because the tiles were falling off. A lack of funds and political will has meant that little other than necessary maintenance has been done on Massey Hall.

The interior is extraordinary. The strong Moorish element in the ceiling is a surprise, the colours are warm and subdued, and the acoustics are astoundingly good. There is not a spot among the twenty-seven hundred seats where you cannot hear the smallest sound from the stage; this large hall gives the impression of intimacy. The magnificent stained-glass windows, depicting various European composers, are mostly boarded up to prevent sound leakage from the street.

Massey Hall has been home to renowned performers, like Artur Rubinstein, Sergei Rachmaninov, Andres Segovia, Glenn Gould, Lois Marshall, Gilles Vigneault and on and on—including Gordon Lightfoot's annual concert over the past three decades. A landmark jazz event took place here on May 15, 1953: some Toronto aficionados invited Max Roach, Dizzy Gillespie, Charlie Parker, Charles Mingus, and Bud Powell, not all of whom customarily played together, for what many critics have labelled the world's greatest jazz concert.

When Roy Thomson Hall (also named after a leading Canadian entrepreneur) opened in the 1980s, there was considerable fear that Massey Hall would be torn down. It has survived but has not received the attention it requires. Present-day audiences desire more commodious crush space and elevators to serve upper floors. Schemes have been advanced to push the front of the building out onto or over Shuter Street but so far have come to naught. Completion of adjacent construction may be the impetus to polish this jewel.

As one of the premier performing spaces in Toronto, Massey Hall has attracted a wide variety of famous personalities other than musicians to its stage, including Winston Churchill, Arthur Conan Doyle, Hilaire Belloc, Grey Owl, André Malraux, Thomas Mann, Nellie McClung, Arthur Miller, and Bertrand Russell. It was also the scene of successful rallies organized in support of the Canadian Communist leader Tim Buck in the 1930s, when the party's reputation was still untarnished.

Max Roach, Dizzy Gillespie and Charlie Parker (with Charles Mingus and Bud Powell present but not shown) at Massey Hall, Toronto, on May 15, 1953.

METROPOLITAN UNITED CHURCH

56 Queen Street East

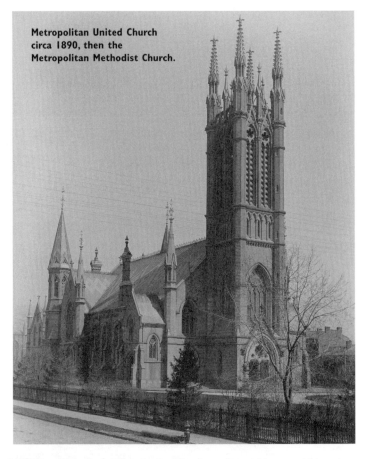

Metropolitan United Church circa 1890, then the Metropolitan Methodist Church.

" **The Cathedral of Methodism**" is how the architectural historian Patricia McHugh refers to this church, competing with St. Michael's Roman Catholic Cathedral immediately to the north, and St. James' Anglican Cathedral several blocks down Church Street.

The common link among the three is Henry Langley, who designed each church tower. In fact, Langley designed the whole of the

Metropolitan Methodist Church, as it was called when it was built in the early 1870s, but the church had a disastrous fire in 1928 and, except for the tower, was rebuilt in a slightly modified form.

A careful look at the tower reveals that Langley had been a trifle more generous with his Gothic detailing than the architect J. Gibb Morton was in the rebuilding of the church in 1929. However, the clear English Gothic elements of the Langley style survive with the side aisles separated by pillars that march along the nave to the deep chancel, and the oak Communion table with a carving that resembles Leonardo da Vinci's *Last Supper*. The church also has the largest pipe organ in Canada (8,233 pipes) and a carillon of fifty-four bells. An iron fence was erected at the edges of the property soon after the church was built, but it was torn down in 1961 when open space and access were deemed more important than protected grounds. The result is that the church's setting has been somewhat destroyed, but the building itself, taken as a whole, has a fine sense of solemnity and order.

In 1925 Canadian Methodists, Congregationalists, and most Presbyterians joined together to form the United Church (hence the change in name). The Church's first general council was held here. During the past few decades, it was one of the first congregations to address social problems in downtown Toronto, sponsoring a program that trained clergy from all denominations to respond positively to downtown residents. One aspect of the program required clergy to spend two or three days on the street living like homeless vagrants. Social programs continue to be a strong part of Metropolitan United's activity, and the homeless problem has grown to such an extent that there are people sleeping on the church grounds on many nights. The church served as the main meeting place for Citizens for Local Democracy (often all twelve hundred seats were filled) as the city struggled against amalgamation in 1997.

The sanctuary.

MORIYAMA & TESHIMA

32 Davenport Road

There is a theory in architecture that certain designs are suitable for certain uses and that the look of a building reflects that purpose. Some have applied that theory to the Summerhill train station on Yonge Street—it has served mostly served as a liquor store in recent decades—claiming it's "really a train station." This theory is confounded by 32 Davenport Road.

This building began life in the 1920s as an automobile service station. The CBC stored equipment here while covering the royal visit of King George VI and Queen Elizabeth in 1939, and at the end of the war it was a beer store. It served various other occupants until 1966, when the current occupants, an architectural firm, moved in and totally renovated the space.

The service station design is difficult to discern from the street. But just inside the door there is a welcoming fish pond—a surprising reinterpretation of the service station's grease pit. Throughout the building there have been many additions and changes over the years, and the space has evolved into something entirely comfortable and airy,

Perhaps the city's most attractive former service station.

The redesigned interior.

brightened by the large skylight in the north section. The building starts out on a single level, but with the changes needed to accommodate a growing staff it has become multi-level and multi-corridored. To use a word that the firm's founder often refers to as the key component of any building, the place has *integrity*.

Raymond Moriyama was born in Vancouver, but, given his Japanese heritage, he was interned during the Second World War by the Canadian government, one of this country's more shameful racist acts. He emerged obviously with fortitude and imagination, and with his partners has made extraordinary contributions to the field of architecture. Notable designs include those for the nearby Toronto Reference Library on Yonge Street, the Scarborough Civic Centre, the Bata Shoe Museum (Bloor and St. George), Science North in Sudbury, and Canadian embassies in Tokyo and Berlin. As he has in the building where he practices, Moriyama often introduces elements of Japanese culture (particularly the calming effect of water) into his designs.

NEW CITY HALL
(TORONTO CITY HALL)

100 Queen Street West

Looking north over Nathan Phillips Square to Toronto City Hall.

Toronto's image as a contemporary city derives from the stunning design of the New City Hall and its square, which was opened in 1965.

In the 1950s, members of City Council were dissatisfied by the civic image projected by their 1899 City Hall on the east side of Bay Street. They wanted a building more expressive of the modern, confident, post-war mood. As well, in 1953 the Metropolitan level of government was established for the million residents of the larger city, creating a federation of the City of Toronto (where 750,000 people then lived), and the small surrounding municipalities that were beginning to explode with suburban growth. Metro Council was responsible for regional issues and large-scale infrastructure such as water and sewage treatment, regional roads, policing, public transit, and social services. The local governments (there were thirteen at the start, but gradually consolidation reduced that number to six) looked after the delivery of services as well as local planning, local roads, recreation, and libraries. Over the ensuing decades, it proved to be an effective way of ensuring that the two competing visions necessary for a healthy city—the regional and the local—found expression and, in spite of obvious in-built tension, resolution. Many believe this two-tier structure of government resulted in the innovations and efficiencies that led, in the 1970s and '80s, to Toronto being called one of the few North American cities that worked.

The City of Toronto commissioned a design for a new city hall that would meet both its and Metro's needs, but when it met opposition, the University of Toronto professor Eric Arthur (who wrote the definitive book on our nineteenth-century architecture, *Toronto, No Mean City*) convinced the councillors that a competition should be held, as had been done for the 1899 city hall. More than five hundred submissions were received from around the world. A condition of competition read as follows: "One of the reasons for this competition is to find a building that will proudly express its function as the centre of civic government. How to achieve an atmosphere about a building that suggests government, continuity of democratic traditions and service to the community are problems for the designer of the modern city hall. These were qualities that the architects of other ages endeavoured to embody in the town halls of their times." The winning design was by Viljo Revell of Finland, and he partnered with Toronto's John C. Parkin to bring the design to reality. (Revell died before the building was completed.) The site was cleared of existing structures, many of which were occupied by members of the city's Chinese community, who moved their businesses north to Dundas Street and, several decades later, west to Spadina Avenue.

The building and the square quickly became the city's proud symbol. The central oyster-shaped structure was the meeting chamber for both City and Metro Councils, and the two towers enclosing the chamber are said to symbolize the two governments. Some internal efficiency is sacrificed for design of the towers: windows on one side and a blank wall (the exterior of which is scalloped, inlaid with marble strips) on the other lead staff to complain of offices being too hot or too cold, too light or too dark. The swooping ceremonial ramp leading up the council chamber is

The Council Chamber, as originally designed, before being renovated for the amalgamated city.

rarely used, as intended, by vehicles. Currently the podium contains a playground (for city hall's workplace day care, which still survives from the optimistic days of the early 1980s) and a running track.

The square is named after Nathan Phillips, mayor when Revell's design was chosen. Phillips was Toronto's first Jewish mayor, serving from 1955 to 1962, and he earned the affectionate sobriquet Mayor of All the People. In the decades after the Second World War, immigrants poured into Toronto, mostly from Europe, and his appearances at community events did much to make disparate groups of Italians, Greeks, Hungarians, and Poles feel this was their city too and that a variety of cultures was something to be prized. Later mayors followed Phillips's lead as immigrants from Southeast Asia, Central and South America, Africa, China, and other countries continued to seek Toronto out. The city has done well by his example—people of many cultures feel at home here. Today, about half of Toronto households have family members born outside Canada.

Nathan Phillips Square created a very popular focal point for civic activity. It remains the location of choice for political demonstrations and for public performances. One reason for its success is its sense of enclosure, created by the elevated walkway that surrounds it and gives the space a protective edge. The growing number of homeless people in the city is sadly reflected here: on an average night, three or four dozen can be found sleeping in the square, some close by the main doors of the City Hall, some in protected spots under the walkway.

The square's reflecting pool becomes a popular skating rink in the winter (this was a happy afterthought of Revell's), but the sundial presented to the city by Phillips is sadly put in shadow from noon onwards by the Sheraton Centre hotel to the south. The city had been concerned that inappropriate development not occur on the south side of Queen Street, so it expropriated the properties—and then encouraged what is seen today, large concrete structures in the brutalist style.

To the west of the main doors to City Hall stands the massive bronze *Three Way Piece No. 2* (known as *The Archer*) by the British sculptor Henry Moore, who subsequently donated a large collection of maquettes, sculptures, and drawings to the Art Gallery of Ontario. *The Archer* figures in "Civil Elegies" by the Toronto poet Dennis Lee (most famous for his children's verse) and a song of the pop singer Murray McLauchlan. The Peace Garden, an unfinished house surrounded by plantings, was constructed in 1985 to coincide with visits by Pope John Paul II (who lit the garden's eternal flame) and Queen Elizabeth.

Just inside the building's main doors to the right is a wall sculpture made of nails, titled *Metropolis*, by David Partridge. It represents the elemental city—a centre surrounded by forms that become less and less dense. A favourite pastime of visiting children is to insert a ten-cent piece near the ceiling and listen to it tinkle its way through the nails to the floor. Past the main information desk is an open area centred by a huge column holding up the Council Chamber. Revell's design originally called for the Council Chamber to rest on the three elevator shafts at the edge of this area, leaving a large open space—what a space it would have been!—but engineers could not find an easy way to distribute the immense weight. The necessary column was made into a virtue: a hallway has been dug out around it, with carpeted stairs descending into a Hall of Memory to Toronto soldiers who died in various wars. The Council Chamber, reached by any of the elevators at the edge of this space, is light and airy, a comfortable and commodious place in which to make decisions about the city. The two tiers of municipal government were abolished in 1997 by the provincial government in a decision that was strongly opposed by most Toronto residents (a plebiscite in March 1997 put the opposition at just over 76 per cent), but the new amalgamated council continues to meet here.

It is worth spending a few minutes in the public areas on the first and second floors to view the city's fine collection of Toronto art. Before amalgamation, the former City of Toronto set aside a modest sum each year to buy works from local artists, and it amassed a collection varied in style and focus. There is a fine bronze of a dockworker (by an exchange artist from Amsterdam) and near the mayor's office an excellent example of the work of one of Canada's foremost aboriginal artists (who often lived in Toronto), Norval Morrisseau.

A view from the second floor of the rotunda's central column, which descends into the Hall of Memory.

OLD CITY HALL

🏛 60 Queen Street West

The best approach to Old City Hall is from the south: walking north on Bay Street, one notes how the building has been carefully designed to provide an impressive vista up the street, with the tower and its clock firmly centred on what's left of the Bay Street canyon formed by the buildings hugging the sidewalk north of

The Bay Street canyon, looking north to City Hall, circa1910.

King Street. (Another example of a building placed specifically to be seen at the end of a street is St. Mary's Roman Catholic Church on Bathurst Street at Adelaide, but unfortunately Adelaide now runs one way east, so the beauty of this church is rarely noticed, save in the rearview mirror.)

In the last few decades of the nineteenth century, the courthouse on Adelaide Street was deemed inadequate, and the city fathers held a competition for the design of a new structure, but it was abandoned because of cost considerations. A second competition was held, and Toronto's E. J. Lennox emerged as the winner. Further delay ensued. The Council decided it also needed a new city hall to replace the one on Front Street. Lennox happily agreed to design something larger and toured American cities seeking inspiration—the Allegheny County Courthouse in Pittsburgh, by the famous American architect H. H. Richardson, apparently had considerable influence.

Construction costs went far over budget, but the building successfully opened in 1899. It has an extraordinary presence—powerful stonework (red stone from the Credit Valley, brown from New Brunswick, grey from Orangeville), graceful but heavy arches, a facade with surface indents and projections and numerous windows creating a rhythm in light and shadow, and copper roofs with green patina. The style is known as Richardson Romanesque.

The facades on all four streets are interesting, but most of the detail is on the Queen Street frontage. On either side of the three massive arches leading to the main doors are friendly lions peering through carved stone foliage. Dragons are recumbent in the V between the arches. Before acid

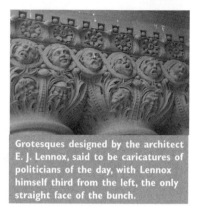

Grotesques designed by the architect E. J. Lennox, said to be caricatures of politicians of the day, with Lennox himself third from the left, the only straight face of the bunch.

rain did its work, gargoyles stuck out from the clock tower, and from just under the roofline. The words "Municipal Building" are found over the arches, reflecting its administrative function. (On Bay Street it reads "Court House" and on James "City Hall," since the former Council Chamber was best accessed through this door.)

The carvings around the groups of three columns on which the arches sit show a fascinating variety of faces, mostly foolish and cartoon-like, said to represent the Council members of the day. There appears to be only one "normal" face, found on the capital of the east columns in the central arch. It's a face of a confident-looking man with a moustache, and it bears a striking similarity to Lennox himself. This is not his only

A City Council meeting, January 11, 1915.

signature on the building: interspersed among the carvings immediately below the ledge of the top row of windows, starting at the northwest corner of the building and working right around, are letters spelling out E J LENNOX ARCHITECT AD 1898.

Inside the clocktower.

Old City Hall now serves as a busy courthouse. Inside the main doors are a half-dozen steps, and straight ahead is one of the few secular stained-glass windows in the city. It shows Commerce extending the hand of friendship to Industry as the smokestacks in the background belch out the nineteenth century's version of progress. The red-and-yellow brick structure in the upper-right quadrant depicts the former city hall on Front Street, now incorporated into the St. Lawrence Market. Turning around and facing the entrance, one notices that the areas between the arches are

The stained-glass window above the grand staircase, showing Commerce greeting Industry (CTA 1244-323).

painted gold and decorated with angels in Pre-Raphaelite style by George Reid, a leading Canadian artist at the turn of the century.

The main hallway is vast, with dark woodwork and a grand staircase. The former Council Chamber is on the second floor of the James Street side of the building, room 121. It currently serves as a courtroom, and its flamboyant and authoritative woodwork is not to be missed. A fine example of nineteenth-century moral style can be found in courtroom 123 in the southwest corner of the building. It is at once severe, proper, and commodious.

In the 1960s, city politicians wanted the building cleared away. Mayor Philip Givens called it "that old dump at Bay and Queen," and he pushed for it to be demolished to make way for the Eaton Centre, a large development of shops and offices. But a group called Friends of the Old City Hall waged a long and tenacious fight to retain the structure, at one point scrubbing away the grime from a small section of the exterior to show its underlying beauty. One of the Friends' few political allies was the controller (and shortly thereafter, mayor) Bill Dennison, who remarked that "if we keep on demolishing our old buildings, there will soon be no evidence that we ever had a past." The Friends finally prevailed in 1966, and the Eaton Centre development scheme was withdrawn, to rebound five years later in a version that did not include demolition of the Old City Hall.

Thus the battle for the Old City Hall was a catalyst for the heritage movement in Toronto. Those who supported it and other heritage buildings also opposed the Spadina Expressway, which would have ripped through downtown residential areas. They wanted to protect rather than destroy neighbourhoods, and they believed in the value of engaging an active citizenry in the decision-making processes at City Hall. These were the new values that gained ascendancy

Toronto Hydro-Electric inauguration at City Hall in 1911 (CTA 1244-323M).

in the early 1970s on City Council, before this legacy was squandered in the late 1990s.

Leaving the building through the main doors, visitors should be sure to pause outside on the steps to take in the Cenotaph honouring the dead in two World Wars; the fine facade of the former Simpson's department store (now the Bay), 1895, designed by Burke and Horwood architects in the Chicago style, after the work of the American architect Louis Sullivan, and the view down Bay Street. William Kurelek, a Toronto artist who painted scenes of daily life in Canada with a religious theme, once created a poignant picture of Christ standing at the top of the steps, unnoticed by the crowds hurrying by on the sidewalk.

ONE KING WEST

1 King Street West

The King Street entrance

This resplendent twelve-storey structure was constructed as the head office of the Dominion Bank in 1912. Designed by the Toronto architecture firm of Darling & Pearson, it exhibits the standard components of tall buildings from the period: it has a base, a middle, and a top, as seen in two other structures sharing the King and Yonge intersection.

The base consists of three storeys of rather plain stone pierced on the Yonge Street side by large arched windows surmounted by a cornice, giving the structure a scale that easily relates to smaller buildings on the street. The King Street entrance is recessed and framed by decorative fluted columns, although glass has been placed between the columns, considerably lessening the impact of the entrance treatment.

The middle section of the building comprises seven floors with simple, regular detailing, and the top two floors are decorated with pilasters separating arched windows and capped with a cornice and balustrade.

The palatial marble staircase inside the main door leads up to the broad, well-proportioned banking hall, where the predominance of grey marble softens the light that flows in from the large arched windows. When the building was originally constructed, great care was taken to ensure that the room was well lit; even the crests on the ceiling were illuminated by hidden lights.

The staircase down from the main entrance opens into a banking vault with a massive circular door, obviously designed to advertise the security of funds on deposit with the bank. The vault is surrounded by a steel grille.

This door—two and a half feet thick, with a weight of thirty tons—opens into a two-storey bank vault.

Mirrors, lights, and reflectors are arranged to permit a guard to have a complete view, including the space underneath the vault, to frustrate those with ideas of tunnelling. The bank advertised that a telephone and instructions were located inside the vault, in the event of a person's being locked in at night, and that fresh air always circulated so there was no danger of asphyxiation.

This structure is part of a redevelopment now under way, which includes a forty-eight-storey tower behind and over it. The banking hall may be used as a performance space for local theatre, and the exterior will remain generally unchanged.

The grand banking hall, with the crest of each province painted in the ceiling panels.

ONTARIO HERITAGE CENTRE

10 Adelaide Street East

When George Gouinlock—born in Paris, Ontario, but active in Toronto from 1888—was commissioned in 1907 to design the headquarters for the Canadian Birkbeck Investment and Savings Company, he seemed to have two things in mind. Most immediate (and not entirely obvious) was the devastating fire Toronto had undergone in 1904, which had destroyed the majority of buildings in the downtown. Gouinlock decided he needed a building well protected from fire, and for this he employed fireproof steel with

terra-cotta infill. His second interest is obvious: Gouinlock had visited the Chicago World's Fair in 1893, where the Beaux-Arts style of architecture was first championed in North America. He was smitten, as the design elements on the exterior of this building show: the lavish decorative work around the arches in the centre of the main facade; the carvings just under the cornices above the fourth floor; the round windows over the doors on each side of the building.

Inside is an attractive two-storey banking hall now used as a meeting space. The door on the right leads past one of the last hand-operated elevators in Toronto to a large two-storey space with a staircase. Each office is partitioned in a way typical of the early decades

10 Adelaide Street East in 1927 (CTA 1244-1086).

The magnificent oval boardroom.

George Gouinlock also designed five buildings for the Canadian National Exhibition, then Canada's premier trade and agriculture show. The Press Building was built in 1904, the Music Building in 1907 (recently restored after an almost fatal fire), the Horticulture Building in 1907, the Government Building in 1912 (now the Liberty Grand), and the fire hall and police station in 1912. This is one of the largest and finest groups of early-twentieth-century exhibition architecture in one location.

of the twentieth century. On the top floor is a handsome panelled boardroom displaying an appropriate degree of solemnity for an investment company of the time. The building was purchased by the Ontario Heritage Foundation in 1985, extensively and lovingly renovated, and now functions as the Foundation's head office.

Gouinlock designed two other important buildings. The Temple Building at Bay and Richmond Streets—the city's first with cast-iron beams and uprights surrounded by concrete to protect them from fire—was an elegant ten-storey structure in the Richardson Romanesque style, with carvings in the red sandstone, including a moose head overlooking the main door and a spacious "bicycle stable" in the basement. It was sadly torn down in 1970 and replaced by an ugly concrete-and-glass structure. (The moose head and the related frieze is preserved in the garden of the Guild Inn in Scarborough.) The second structure by Gouinlock is an entirely different style: the north wing of the Legislative Building in Queen's Park, which serves as the Legislative Library.

ONTARIO LEGISLATIVE BUILDING

Queen's Park (College Street and University Avenue)

This is the fourth legislative structure for Ontario, following the first at Parliament and Front Streets burned down by American soldiers in 1813; a second at the same location; and a third from the 1830s at King and Simcoe Streets.

The present building, erected on the site of a former lunatic asylum, was the result of an international competition in 1880. Its jury of three members, including the Buffalo architect R. A. Waite, made first and second choices, although when each one estimated that the cost would exceed government estimates, they were asked to prepare working drawings from which firmer estimates were made. Both proposals were considered too expensive, and the idea was put aside. But the cramped conditions in the King and Simcoe structure meant the government was unable to prevaricate too long, and in 1885 Waite was asked to choose between the two proposals. Instead, he chose himself, stating that he was "the only architect on the continent capable of carrying out such important work." Surprisingly, he was elevated from the position of jury member to architect for the new building. The cost of his structure was over $1.2 million, more than double the most expensive estimate of either of the unsuccessful bidders.

Like many legislatures, this one is in a park-like setting disconnected from the life of the city, a characteristic some would say is deliberate and often reflected in the body's decisions. It is a bulky, thick building whose weight seems exaggerated by the profusion of red Credit Valley stone. At first glance the central block, with its Middle Eastern domes and high-pitched roof seems symmetrical, but the side towers differ considerably in detailing. The wings on either side also vary, but this is because the western portion, designed by E. J. Lennox, replaces what was destroyed by fire in the early twentieth century.

The arches over and columns between the main door seem to bear a heavy load that is in no way lightened by the large arched windows of the Assembly Chamber, the circular windows above, or the dormer at the base of the roof.

Corridor to the.Legislative Library, circa 1912 (CTA 1244-1131).

Inside the main doors is a wide foyer and yawning hallways, then a cascading staircase leading up to the second floor. On the second floor, the Assembly Chamber itself is finely decorated with wooden carvings and ironwork, but here too the general theme is heaviness. Even the recently uncovered painted ceiling decoration and wooden beams add to the ponderousness not found in most other late-Victorian buildings in Toronto.

The wings to either side of the central block are largely open atriums, surrounded at each level by ornamental ironwork. Many interesting artworks are hung throughout the buildings, including drawings by C. W. Jefferys—on the second floor of the east wing—of the rebels marching down Yonge Street in 1837. An exceptional painting by George Reid of a mortgage foreclosure—a sick farmer lies in his bed close to death, his young wife rocks a baby in a cradle at his side, as the children stand wondering about their future— is on the north wall of second floor, west wing.

The Amethyst Room on the first floor just to the left of the main staircase has recently been renovated in the Victorian style, with captivating colours and a considerable lightness of touch. The committee rooms on the first floor of the west wing are plainer and more robust, with heavy wooden panelling.

The east and west wing entrances appear to belong to the late nineteenth-century: one can picture horsedrawn carriages arriving under the heavy porte cochère at the bottom of the steps. The north section on Wellesley Street was designed by George Gouinlock and completed two decades after the main structure. Its entrance is surrounded by stone carvings like the Ontario Coat of Arms, above which two large lions spit at each other, and several Celtic panels.

The entrance to the lieutenant-governor's suite is found at the northwest corner of the building. Just outside its door is a sculpture by Walter Allward commemorating William Lyon Mackenzie and the struggle for social justice. Other sculptures are sprinkled in front of the building. In front of the main entrance are a number of statues: George Brown, publisher of *The Globe* and a father of Confederation, and Sir Oliver Mowat, Liberal premier of Ontario from 1872 to '96 and a proponent of provincial rights, are to the west; to the east are John Sandfield MacDonald, premier from 1867 to '71, a stern, seated Queen Victoria and Sir James Whitney, premier from 1904 to '14. On the far east side of the park is a light and lovely memorial to those who died putting down the Northwest (Riel) Rebellion in 1885.

A third-floor corridor, as photographed circa 1893.

OSGOODE HALL

 130 Queen Street West

To many in Toronto, Osgoode Hall (named after William Osgoode, the first chief justice of Ontario) is something of a mystery, protected from prying eyes by its high iron fence. In fact, much of the structure is open to the public.

The library (CTA 1244-3153).

The central section, seen here, was an addition to Osgoode Hall, built in 1857 of Berea sandstone.

It serves as the centre of senior court activities for Ontario, with courtrooms for appeals, procedural motions, and other activities that are usually only attended by lawyers, as well as offices for judges. It also holds the offices of the Law Society of Upper Canada, which governs the activities of lawyers, as well as the Society's main law library. In the northeast corner are the facilities for the bar admission course, the final step required of students before they're called to the bar. The province's first law school was located here (University of Toronto established a second school in 1957) until it became affiliated with York University in 1969.

The formidable iron fence was designed in 1866 by William Storm and cast in a Toronto foundry from moulds made in Scotland. The fence has survived numerous attempts at removal, including a move to use it to meet an iron shortage in the Second World War and the dream of traffic engineers to widen Queen Street in the 1960s. The complicated way through the fence is a means to keep cows out, since the lush grass within was an attraction to the neighbouring beasts. Note the beavers on the top of the main gate on the south side. Inside the fence is an oasis of grassy space, too rare in the central city.

What is now the east wing of Osgoode was the original building, completed in 1832. The classical portico was added later, around 1844, when the centre was reconstructed and the west wing was built. In the late 1850s, the middle section was replaced and a central portico was added to mimic those on either side, totally changing the look. It has weathered well, and today feels, to many of those who use it, all of one piece.

Doors Open participants gather in the rotunda, around a Second World War memorial statue.

The interior is outstanding, with many gorgeous elements. Through the main doors is the richly patterned tiled floor, with the same engaging red, black and tawny tiles found in George Brown House and University College. One is drawn immediately through to the loggia, where honey-coloured stone is bathed in delicate pink light in a space that Henry Scadding, the nineteenth-century historian of Toronto said "reminded him of a Genoese palace." It is surely one of the most engaging spaces in Toronto, and the artist Cleeve Horne's statue of mother and child, a Second World War memorial, is an appealing addition to the peaceful place. Courtrooms 8, 9, and 10, on either side of the loggia, each offer a different design expression of the majesty of justice: one is strong blue and red, another a faded yellow and brown, another olive green.

Walk back a few paces to the grand stairway, which ascends on both sides, and climb the blue-carpeted steps under the portraits of former judges. At the top of the stairs visitors will find themselves standing beneath a fine skylight with stained glass, forced to choose between a breathtaking view of the loggia from the second floor and the doors to the Great Library. The library is an extraordinary room, although some might say that it fails at its main tasks: the etched windows on the south side produce a glare that does not aid reading, and the plaster-work and pillars are of such high quality that it seems unfair to intrude on this space with bookcases. But these are minor failures—the space is overpowering—grand, serious, full of the rational light of the law. The space is a triple cube: 40 feet wide, 40 feet high, and 120 feet long.

The fireplace at the west end is large enough to walk into, and behind it is a pleasant room with a cork floor and a spiral staircase leading to an upper level of books. At the east end of the library is a Carrera marble figure memorializing the First World War, replacing a stained-glass window. From either end of the room one takes in the numerous fluted Corinthian columns, the vaulted coffered ceilings in the cube vaults, the central dome, the pediment over the main door, the clarity of the light.

Out of the library, wander around the upper level of the loggia to look at Courtrooms 1, 5, and 6, just as distinguished as those on the main floor. And there's more. Walk east on the corridor to the Benchers' quarters. Like other professionals in Ontario, lawyers are self-governing, controlled by the Law Society of Upper Canada, and its board of directors—the Benchers—are elected by Ontario lawyers. Their quarters are in the east wing, which contains a marvellous glass dome, an oak staircase, a sedate meeting room, and a dining room that has what is reputed to be one of the finest wine cellars in the

> Following the Rebellion in December 1837, the government leased Osgoode Hall for use as a military barracks until it was clear that the rebellious elements were fully put down. The troops stayed from June 1838 for a full five years, leaving the building in such poor condition that the government was required to pay the Society the very large sum of 480 pounds to restore order.

The fireplace in the Osgoode Hall library, circa 1910 (CTA 1244-310).

country. The Society's seal—a beaver separating Hercules from the blindfolded Justice—is kept here. Farther along the hallway is the baronial Convocation Hall with stained-glass windows tracing law's development through the ages. Larger meetings of the Society are held here, and its members may gather for lunch.

Osgoode Hall demands regular visits, at least once a year, by every friend of Toronto. It remains one of the most engaging, although perhaps least appreciated, of the city's architectural treasures.

ROSEWATER SUPPER CLUB
(FORMER CONSUMERS GAS COMPANY BUILDING)

 19 Toronto Street

In the 1870s David Dick (who later gained fame for his restoration of University College in 1890, after it burned down) designed the head office of the Consumers Gas Company, which since its founding in 1848 had become Toronto's chief supplier of gas.

The Consumers Gas building is now home to the stylish Rosewater Supper Club. Most of what you see here is actually an addition, built in 1899, twenty-five years after the original structure.

The architecture was meant to reflect the company's substance and status. The stone is honey-coloured, and the regularly placed large windows become more elaborately decorative with every storey: from simple polished granite columns between windows on

The front lounge.

the main floor and decorated arches above, to fluted pilasters on the second, and a profusion of detail, including carved keystones on the third.

In 1899 an addition of two new doorways and the three bays on the upper floors was so effectively made to the south of the original structure that today it is difficult to identify these later sections. The building has now been converted into a restaurant and the interior transformed. The ceiling of painted ceramic mouldings and beams rises above hardwood floors on strong red marble columns, and the interior is divided into a series of spaces that create a comfortable ambience. A waterfall spills appealingly over a portion of the north wall. The original occupant's company name may still be seen below the first-floor exterior cornice, as well as at the rear, viewed from Court House Square.

Across the street at 36 Toronto Street is a fine office building designed by E. J. Lennox (the architect of the Old City Hall) manifesting the pre-1950s style of tall buildings with a base (the first two floors, delineated by a cornice), a middle (the intervening stories), and a top. In this case the top has Corinthian pillars under a strong cornice.

Farther to the south at 10 Toronto Street is the former Seventh Post Office, bearing considerable resemblance to the courthouse on Adelaide Street, although the fluted Ionic columns and the sculpted crest on the roof give the building a much lighter touch. Both structures were designed by Cumberland & Ridout; the Post Office was built in the early 1850s and today is occupied by a holding company controlled by Conrad Black, a leading Canadian newspaper mogul until he gave up his Canadian citizenship to become an English peer, Lord Black of Crossharbour.

LE ROYAL MERIDIEN KING EDWARD HOTEL

37 King Street East

In the late nineteenth century there was nowhere in Toronto grand and respectable enough to put up visiting dignitaries. The Queen's Hotel on Front and York Streets had been around for more than six decades and was in poor condition, and the Rossin House Hotel at King and York Streets was considered out of fashion.

Three businessmen of the day—George Jarvis, George Copps of the Bank of Commerce, and George Gooderham of Gooderham and Worts—created the Toronto Hotel Company and chose the King

The "King Eddy", 1903.

Street site of the Golden Lion Clothing Store (a statue of a golden lion sat on the parapet above the main entrance) as the location of their new enterprise. This was once the site of the city's first jail as well.

E. J. Lennox, architect of Old City Hall, was retained to design the structure that finally saw construction start in late 1901. The optimism was

The spectacular main lobby and mezzanine.

such that as construction proceeded, a decision was made to add two more storeys—they are clad in stone and embellished with frilly carvings, emphasizing the elegance of the top of the structure.

The entrance, now overshadowed by a large blue awning, is framed by a powerful stone arch, above which is a bay window. The grade level on King Street consists of shops, and the cornice creates a simple visual break from the storeys above. The corner space at King and Victoria is particularly appealing, with its columns and glass. While the building is largely brick, the window openings are decorated with stone so that as a piece it looks respectable and dignified, if perhaps overly formal.

The main entrance opens into an expansive column-filled lobby with a mezzanine and a skylight. The plushness of the carpet underfoot and the large comfortable lounge chairs are entirely appropriate to this grand and refined space. Café Victoria is an Edwardian room, with large arched windows and lavish decoration. The words of the publicist describing the hotel when it opened apply to this room: "elegant enough in style to serve as the boudoir of a Pompadour were its dimensions not so vast." To the immediate left of the entranceway is a warm and inviting bar, with a dark wood floor and the gleam of brass and sparkling glassware, where guests can calmly look through the large windows at the passing crowds on King Street.

Café Victoria, designated a historical site in 1975 .

In the early days of the King Edward Hotel, a room without bath could be had for $1.50 a night. It has attracted a succession of famous guests—Mark Twain, Lloyd George, Enrico Caruso, Anna Pavlova, Rudolph Valentino, the Prince of Wales who abdicated and then came to stay as the Duke of Windsor, the Beatles, Yoko Ono, and the Queen Mother.

The staircase to the second floor is immediately beside the bar. From the mezzanine, the view of the lobby is of a sumptuous setting. At the south end of this floor is the Vanity Fair Ballroom, with two chandeliers twinkling in its barrel vault sitting on creamy marble columns. Palm Court, on the other side of the lobby, originally served as the women's lounge, just as the door on the first floor from Victoria Street was considered to be the women's entrance.

The hotel was such a success that in 1917 a sixteen-storey addition was built on the east side. The shops in this new structure create a real continuity along King Street, but the upper floors of the tower have none of the grace of the original hotel. The addition, which can best be viewed from Leader Lane, is in two sections linked by an arch at the upper floors, providing easy access to the Crystal Ballroom on the top floor. The large windows served the ballroom, which has not been open to the public since the late 1970s.

The King Edward was one of the best hotels in Toronto until the 1970s, when it began to fall into decline. In the early 1980s, following renovation plans prepared by the American firm of Jutris & Nobili, the interior space was entirely reworked, and the 470 rooms were reconfigured to create 350 much larger rooms and suites. The hotel has now regained its original cachet. Plans are under way for further room renovation in honour of the hotel's one-hundredth anniversary in May 2003.

ST. GEORGE'S GREEK ORTHODOX CHURCH

115 Bond Street

In 1897 the Jewish community built a magnificent synagogue called Holy Blossom, and it is this building that is now known as St. George's Greek Orthodox Church. When Holy Blossom Synagogue moved in 1937 to follow the Jewish community north and west up Bathurst Street, it left this structure in the hands of a congregation that has shown the building great respect and care.

The exquisite iconographic frescoes, which replicate well-known masterpieces of Byzantine art from Constantinople, Greece and Serbia, were painted by Pachomaioi monks.

A strong Romanesque arch presides over the two main doors, flanked by heavy pillars on either side. The two large domes at the north and south ends of the facade have been adapted somewhat by the new congregation to become less Moorish than formerly. The tympanum—a semi-circular space between a lintel and an arch—originally identified the site as Holy Blossom Synagogue, with Hebrew lettering and in English, "Hear, O Israel, the Lord Our God, the Lord Is One." This area has been covered by a mosaic of St. George slaying the dragon.

Inside the building one sees that this is not a square structure but octagonal, with four columns holding up the central dome pierced by clerestory windows, through which sunlight pours down. The white walls are adorned with brilliant panels of saints and angels elaborated with gold leaf. Much of this decoration occurred during renovations in 1980, when Pachomaioi monks, iconographers from Mount Athos in Greece, were retained for the purpose. Their painting duplicates Byzantine master-pieces from Constantinople (now Istanbul) from the fourteenth and fifteenth centuries. St. George's is the only church on the continent to be so decorated. The iron grille work around the balcony is of a high quality. The space is both intimate and uplifting.

Established in 1909, the Greek Orthodox parish of St. George is the oldest Greek Orthodox community in Canada. The church was originally the Holy Blossom synagogue, the oldest surviving synagogue in the city.

Evidently different religions had no problem with close proximity in places of worship. Directly across the street stands the first Lutheran church in Toronto, occupying a small stucco structure from 1899. St. Michael's Roman Catholic Cathedral is less than a block to the south.

ST. JAMES' CATHEDRAL

Corner of King and Church Streets

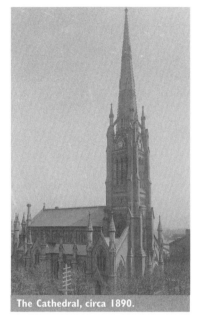

The Cathedral, circa 1890.

A fire in the heart of the city in 1849 destroyed St. James' Cathedral, as well as other buildings on King Street, such as the first City Hall. Apparently the fire began in the out-buildings behind Graham's Tavern on King Street and spread rapidly.

The marble baptismal font in the west vestibule is the only item to survive and find a home in the present cathedral. To rebuild, the congregation held a competition, and Frederic W. Cumberland was chosen to design the new church—his first major commission in Toronto (he had arrived from England in 1847), to be followed by many other notable buildings such as University College, additions to Osgoode Hall, and the Chapel of St. James-the-Less.

The congregation was divided on whether the new building would have the character of a parish church or a cathedral but ultimately decided on the latter. Cumberland designed a structure in the English Gothic Revival mode. It is said that the design was inspired by Trinity Church on Wall Street in New York City, built a few years earlier, although there is a resemblance, at a much more modest scale, to elements of Salisbury Cathedral in England. Unlike most cathedrals, which have the altar at the east end, this one is oriented north. Most of the construction is of local yellow brick: the expense of stone meant it was only used for significant design elements such as the magnificent main door with its projecting pillars, mouldings, and window frames. From the exterior the church is handsome and imposing.

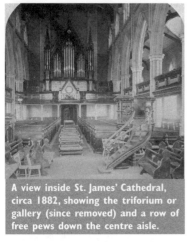

A view inside St. James' Cathedral, circa 1882, showing the triforium or gallery (since removed) and a row of free pews down the centre aisle.

Inside, the ceiling is heavily timbered, the walls are white, and tall, elegant groups of columns support the pointed arches of the nave. Originally there were balconies along the side aisles, happily since removed to make the church more open and airy than Cumberland had designed. The chancel ceiling is painted in a delicate embroidery-like style, and the tripartite stained-glass windows are dazzling with exceptional clarity of light and colour. Just before the altar is the burial place of Bishop John Strachan. He was a member of the Family Compact, the powerful group that controlled decisions in Upper Canada in the first four decades of the nineteenth century. This was their church, and if Strachan had had his way, it would have been the Established Church of Upper Canada. Needless to say, he pursued a hostile relationship with the reformer William Lyon Mackenzie.

Many plaques and interesting window designs are found throughout the church. The stained-glass north window on the east aisle was dedicated to William Jarvis, patriarch of the prominent Jarvis family early in the nineteenth century. The grave marker of the surveyor-general Thomas Ridout, found in the south vestibule, has particularly beautiful carvings, and beside it is the memorial to his son John, who was killed in a duel with Samuel Jarvis, son of William. Nearby is the memorial to William Butcher, a worker who fell from the spire of the previous St. James' Cathedral during construction.

The cathedral opened in 1853. Although funds were exhausted, the tower had not yet been completed. Money was later found from insurance proceeds and from selling pews (hence it became confirmed as a church for the well-to-do). In 1866 construction was completed on a thirty-four-foot tower designed by William Storm. Seven years later the spire was completed to plans of Henry Langley, who had also designed towers for Metropolitan United and St. Michael's Cathedral; at 314 feet it remains the highest in Canada, on the continent second only to the spire on St. Patrick's Roman Catholic Cathedral in New York. The clock in the tower—a gift of the citizens of Toronto—has been maintained for more than a century on a grant from the city.

The fence that originally marked the perimeter of the property has been taken down, and to the east the city has created a large park by purchasing and demolishing commercial structures and closing Market Street, which ran north from King Street to Adelaide, just west of Jarvis. A bandshell has been erected in the middle of the park, among the grassy knolls. With the gutting of social housing programs over the past decade, some of the immense number of the city's homeless people live in this park. Their occupancy has generally reduced its use by others. The Toronto Garden Club maintains the fenced-in flower garden on the north side of King, just east of Church. On the west side of the church is a monument resembling an English cross, a memorial to congregants who died in the First and Second World Wars.

Immediately across King Street from the cathedral is a sculpture garden, a gift of the Toronto businessman Lou Odette, featuring displays of contemporary sculpture. Walk through the garden, then through the courtyard dividing two sections of the Market Square condominium complex: turning around, one is surprised and delighted to find that these buildings have been designed to provide a remarkable and striking view of the cathedral from Front Street.

The nave.

ST. JAMES' PARISH HOUSE ARCHIVES AND MUSEUM

65 Church Street

When St. James' Cathedral was built during the mid-nineteenth century, much of this land had been used for burial purposes. The Parish House was built around 1910—replacing a school erected in 1862—in a style that reflects the Gothic arches and yellow brick of the cathedral, but in a decidedly more modest fashion. The addition on Church Street is from the mid-twentieth century. The building is used for church activities and the diocese office.

But the structure houses a remarkable archive and museum. Materials date back to the founding of the Anglican Church in Upper Canada, including many items relating directly to John Strachan, rector of the church, and then bishop of the diocese in the 1840s until his death in 1867. A portion of the Parish House has been rented to the C. D. Howe Institute, a foundation advising government of the views of corporate leaders. C. D. Howe was a Canadian businessman and politician who held several ministerial portfolios in the federal Liberal government in the 1940s and 1950s.

Serious discussions were held throughout 2000 and 2001 about rebuilding the Parish House and constructing a large private condominium on adjacent land to the northeast. This proposal raised considerable controversy on two issues: first, whether a new structure could be appropriately designed not to interfere with views of the cathedral from the south (proponents of the condominium argued that a tower could be built to the north and east of the cathedral outside important sightlines, but opponents doubted that outcome); second, whether the church should be entering a financial arrangement with a developer. Church officials argued that without significant funds for renovation, the building itself would be in peril and there was no other easy way to generate the monies needed.

An added issue was the remains of some of the victims of the 1834 cholera epidemic in which both Bishop Strachan and William Lyon Mackenzie played a personal role helping the sick and dying. Construction would require that the bodies be exhumed from the Parish House grounds, which would be costly and would require special approvals from provincial officials who oversee cemeteries. The issue was resolved when the cathedral received a large bequest, which allowed the cathedral to consider other options.

ST. LAWRENCE HALL
(CITIZENS FOR THE OLD TOWN)

 157 King Street East

The fire in 1849 that destroyed most of the city's commercial district on King Street, including St. James' Cathedral, also created the opportunity for the building of St. Lawrence Hall. The architect William Thomas had been retained in 1845 to design a new building along the north side of Market Square. Thomas's plans were impressive, but the cost was too high.

Then came the fire. Thomas's plans were revived and St. Lawrence Hall was the result. The sixteenth-century Italian classicist architect Andrea Palladio was the clear influence: a central section sports four Corinthian columns on the second and third storeys over three arches forming the entrance; this leads up to a pediment above the third floor; above that is a square attic with a balustrade; and on the very top are tall white columns holding up a small dome with clocks facing each direction. The windows are classically sedate, perfectly proportioned. To either side of this fine central section are superb three-storey wings with delicate ironwork at the second floor level.

The stone is a warm honey colour, and there is enough detail (carved by Scottish craftsmen) in swags, wreathes, masks, and remarkable, intricate carving to satisfy the sensuous eye as it moves along the surface of the building. The stone carving of the city arms in the pediment is a fine work, even when viewed from the distance of the sidewalk. The shopfronts to either side are glass, making the central portion of the building even more prominent.

The keystone head over the main entrance is thought to represent the god of the St. Lawrence, and the name has been stuck to other undertakings by the city, including a nearby theatre and new neighbourhood—while the other two heads represent the gods of Niagara

The Hall in 1867.

and Lake Ontario. William Dendy catches it just right when he says in his book *Toronto Observed* that this structure bridges the city's late-Georgian heritage and the confident Victorian character.

Activities of great public interest took place in the Great Hall. This ballroom on the third floor was prized for its ceiling, decorated with ornamental plaster and gold leaf, and its grand gas-lit chandelier. It became the city's most fashionable venue for several decades in the mid-nineteenth century—the crowds came for balls, lectures (the American poet and essayist Ralph Waldo Emerson spoke here), concerts (Jenny Lind sang), and political events (Sir John A. Macdonald and D'Arcy McGee appeared). The event that opened the building, on April 1, 1851, was a lecture on the abolition of slavery in the United States.

In time, the allure of St. Lawrence Hall faded, particularly as new structures like Massey Hall were built. By the turn of the twentieth century, the upper storeys of the building were little used, and they sat almost vacant for fifty years. In 1951 the National Ballet of Canada established its home on the second floor, and that proved to be the building's salvation. As a project marking Canada's Centennial in 1967, City Council decided to renovate in the face of loud criticism from the media, which preferred that the building be demolished to make way for the future. But the City persevered in its plans, even when part of the structure collapsed in the midst

St. Lawrence Hall after the disastrous collapse caused by workers who cut almost completely through supporting wall joists during its 1967 restoration.

of renovation (miraculously, no one was injured), and the hall's elegance was restored. The project refocused attention on this significant area where the city was founded. Only a few years later, the south St. Lawrence Market building was renovated rather than torn down, and construction began on the successful St. Lawrence community to the south.

The original entrance way.

As for the Town of York, the Citizens for the Old Town (located in the building) are working to give prominence to what remains of it. The original town laid out by Alexander Aitkin, under the instruction of Lieutenant-Governor John Graves Simcoe in 1793, was five blocks (from Jarvis to Berkeley Streets) by two blocks (Front to Adelaide). The Citizens have pressed for recognition of the Old Town, leading the fight to undertake the archeological dig at Parliament and Front Streets that uncovered the remains of the Parliament buildings burned down by the Americans in the War of 1812. They lobby to ensure development is appropriate to the structures in the town and that historical elements are given due recognition. It seems strange that so much energy is needed to protect and enhance Toronto's heritage, but sadly, as the Citizens know, that seems to be the reality in today's city.

And the group has had some successes. The new residential buildings at Jarvis and King Streets agreeably conform to the scale and feel of St. Lawrence Hall, as do the Market Square condominium buildings to the west and the commercial ones on King Street facing St. James' Park.

TORONTO–DOMINION CENTRE

🏛 55 King Street West

The main banking pavilion, with the lower floors of two enormous towers visible behind it.

The black glass-and-steel towers of the Toronto–Dominion Centre constitute the first International Style project in the heart of the downtown and are, as the Toronto writer John Bentley Mays says, "intellectually and aesthetically compelling."

In 1955 the Toronto and the Dominion Banks merged, and the consolidation of their properties resulted in a large site at the southwest corner of King and Bay Streets. The Bronfman family were investors in the Toronto–Dominion Centre project and had recently completed their Seagram Building in New York City. Sam Bronfman's daughter, Phyllis Lambert, an architect and patron of the arts, had previously secured Ludwig Mies van der Rohe, a defining architect of the International

Style, to design the Seagram Building, and her influence meant that Mies was retained again in the early 1960s for this site.

An assumption of the International Style was that older buildings would be cleared from the site, allowing the architect to proceed tabula rasa, with new structures obliterating any sense of the past.

Demolition on the TD site was one of the first examples of large-scale clearance in the downtown. This particular city block contained a number of interesting older structures, including the 1912 head office of the Bank of Toronto, at the southwest corner of King and Bay Streets. A small model of this building can be found in the northwest corner of the new banking pavilion that replaces it. One can see how fine were its three-storey fluted Corinthian columns and the human scale that it respected, though it was an imposing structure. The model unfortunately does not reveal the interior brasswork or the various colours of marble that decorated the interior.

On the cleared site, Mies designed two office towers (the higher at fifty-five storeys) and a single-

The Bank of Toronto, corner of King and Bay Streets
Toronto, Canada

The former Bank of Toronto on the site was demolished to make way for the present structure. Remnants of the old bank were salvaged and are displayed on the grounds of the Guild in Scarborough.

storey pavilion, all set on a broad plaza. Not surprisingly, the TD Centre resembles the Seagram Building, having the same facade, wall covering in the main lobbies, and lighting fixtures. The one-storey banking pavilion near the southwest corner of King and Bay has an elegant simplicity both inside and out, with well-proportioned interior space, marvellously hued wood and green marble, and a subtle warm light. A third tower has been added on the south side of Wellington Street (see sidebar). (The tower over the Design Exchange on Bay Street is not a Mies design and not formally part of the project.)

Retail and other street activity have been relegated to an underground shopping mall where, until very recently, individual propri-

Inside the main banking pavilion a warm light spills over the polished wood and marble, as well as the customers.

etors were required to adhere to a uniform signage identity established by Mies and enforced by management. Relocating pedestrian traffic ensures pristine open plazas aboveground, thus enhancing the inhuman scale of the towers. John Bentley Mays identifies the project's key characteristics as "the vast indifference of the project to human scale, however defined; the unrelenting impersonality of the soaring walls of glass and blackened steel; the dramatically vacant intervals among the buildings. . . ."

Mies went to considerable lengths to make his buildings feel plain and flat. The exterior walls of the banking pavilion and the towers are lined with protruding metal that help create the monumental feel.

On the King Street plaza, a circular bronze sculpture with chairs (titled *Wall and Chairs*) by Al McWilliams has been installed as a work of conceptual art. Beside the Wellington Street tower are gentle bronze cows, created by the Regina artist Joe Fafard, grazing on a postage stamp of grass. These graceful creatures relate indirectly to more exotic carved beasts on many buildings from the 1920s and '30s still remaining on Bay Street, north of King.

The Aetna Tower at 79 Wellington Street West, added to the TD Centre, contains a gallery on the second floor that is a treasure trove of Inuit art. More than two hundred sculptures, drawings, and paintings by Inuit artists are on display. The collection was originally assembled for Canada's 1967 Centennial celebrations, and the permanent gallery was established two decades later.

Mies's singular vision is apparent when the TD Centre is compared with less inspired office buildings from the same period: the 1958 Prudential building at the northwest corner of King and Yonge Streets; the 1961 Sun Life building at 196 University Avenue; and the 1958 federal government building on Adelaide Street east of Yonge, since renovated.

TORONTO HARBOUR COMMISSIONERS ADMINISTRATION BUILDING
(TORONTO PORT AUTHORITY)

60 Harbour Street

Today this building looks high and dry, but when erected in 1917 it stood at the water's edge, and large sailing ships tied right up by its front door. In those days there was booming port activity in Toronto, which served as an important harbour on the Great Lakes.

The Toronto Harbour Commissioners Administration Building, before landfill moved the shoreline south (CTA 1244-3178).

Four decades later, when the St. Lawrence Seaway opened, the expectation was that port activity would expand, but that future proved illusory: with the advent of containers for transporting goods, shipping into Toronto was no longer essential. Today, harbour activity is very limited, save for recreational sailing.

The Harbour Commissioners building has been stranded by more than a century's dumping of landfill into the bay. In the 1850s, Front Street marked the bay's shore (the gentle fall of

The boardroom, one of Canada's finest.

roads crossing Front Street indicate the former water's edge), but fill generated by the excavation required to provide footings for large office towers has pushed the water's edge farther and farther out, until today it extends another hundred yards south of this building. (Since the mid-1960s, most fill has been used to create the Leslie Street spit, begun as a Harbour Commission project to create an outer harbour to accommodate shipping activity that never arrived.)

The fine Beaux-Arts columns of the structure, designed by Alfred Chapman, rise from a base over the first floor and hold up the entablature that identifies the building, spelling *Harbor* in the American style, without the *u*. The stone coat of arms over the door incorporates two hopeful angels apparently sitting in a vegetable or grape harvest. Just inside the door is a fine coffered ceiling. An elegant boardroom panelled in walnut, with a large fireplace, occupies part of the second floor.

The Harbour Commission, or Port Authority, as it is now known, has displayed considerable difficulty aligning its decisions with the policies of Toronto City Council, perhaps because the board is appointed by the federal government. In the confusion over whose interests should best be served, most of the land managed by the Port Authority remains vacant and underused, a sad contrast to this distinguished structure.

UNION STATION

65 Front Street West

The Great Hall features a Gustavino tile ceiling and Zumbro (Missouri) stone walls.

Union Station is Canada's temple to transportation. Construction began in 1914 on behalf of the Grand Trunk Railway and the Canadian Pacific Railway, but the economic drain of the First World War, followed by the financial collapse of the Grand Trunk Railway in 1919 (it was replaced by the Canadian National Railways), meant that the station was not completed for a decade. Problems with track alignment further delayed the opening by the Prince of Wales to 1927, although serious use of the facility did not begin until 1930.

The station's principal architect was John M. Lyle, and what a fine building he created. Its design and interior details show the Beaux-Arts influence. The long facade on Front Street is divided into several sections, the central one a massive Doric colonnade flanked by two small projecting porticos. The ground floor features a vast hall for ticket windows and services under a vaulted coffered ceiling eighty-eight feet high. The names of many Canadian destinations are carved in a frieze high on the walls. This expansive space is an entirely appropriate repository for the memories of soldiers leaving for Europe in the Second World War and the joyful reunions of those who returned, as well as of the many immigrants who emerged tired and bewildered to start a new life here after travelling halfway around the world. The hall is flooded with natural light during the day, both through the windows high along the front and back and from windows in the arches at either end.

The building now functions primarily as a transfer point between commuter rail (with fifty such trains a day) and the subway. Intercity rail has been discouraged for many years in Canada, and that business here is slim, no more than a handful of trains a day.

In spite of its splendour, the building has endured a number of threats to its existence. In the early 1970s, when train travel was no longer in favour, City Council was bent on facilitating a major redevelopment on the two hundred acres of railway lands and called for the station's destruction. A momentous fight between citizens and City Council ensued (comparable to the fight over the Old City Hall a decade earlier), and the project was defeated. The current City Council is once again thinking of redevelopment options to intensify the use of the structure.

A view of a walkway just in front of the station's main doors.

WHITNEY BLOCK

99 Wellesley Street West

With the expansion of government in Canada following the First World War, the need for an administrative building for provincial employees in Ontario became apparent. Even with its additions, the Legislative Building was not large enough for a burgeoning bureaucracy.

Francis Heakes designed the Whitney Block, the province's first administrative building, which opened in 1928. Most of this seven-storey structure is grey sandstone, not organized as a block but in a series of wings to ensure that offices were well supplied with natural light. Since the 1950s that has not been the style for office buildings: the floor plates of Modern-style buildings are so large that most employees work in artificial light. In Germany, much attention is given to the proximity of workers to natural light, and regulations are being developed there to restrict the distance of any space from a window. If such regulations came to Ontario, the Whitney Block would be the model to follow.

The basement floor has been raised so that its windows are above ground, and the main floor is a half-dozen steps above grade. Bands of stone separate the main floor from what is below and above. As well, the top floor contains much decorative stonework below the cor-

A marble hallway.

nice. It is not a tall building for its time, but it has been designed to have a base, a middle, and a top, in discrete sections like those at Yonge and King Street built during the same period.

The doorways are all recessed and flanked by narrow columns under a strict pediment. The main floor windows have a modified Gothic touch, and the whole impression is one of clean and rather hard lines.

The tower was designed by George White after Heakes's death and was begun in the early years of the Depression. While it uses the same materials as the main building, it seems to be hidden away toward the south of the complex, without the prominence that perhaps it should have. It rises in a wedding-cake style, studded with sculptures carved in situ by Charles Adamson. At the corners on the sixteenth floor, beginning at the southeast and moving clockwise, are the statues of Justice, Tolerance, Power, and Wisdom. All are female. On the twelfth floor are eight men—two on each side—depicting various depart-

Charles Adamson, a Toronto sculptor, carved twelve allegorical figures on the tower in situ during 1933, each representing a skill valued by the government of the day.

ments of the government: finance and health on the south, farming and forestry on the west, labour and mining on the north, law and education on the east. This was obviously an era when government had pride in the enterprise of ordinary people and saw its function as serving them. How the world turns!

The interior of the building has been renovated to enhance the sense that it is an office building from the 1920s and 1930s. The floor is made of different coloured tiles, and elevator banks have modest brass detailing and bronze doors. When the building was new, there was a bowling alley in the basement, along with ice-making facilities.

James Whitney, after whom this building was named, was the premier of Ontario from 1905 to 1914. He led a progressive government that established Ontario's publicly owned hydroelectric system, passed legislation to provide compensation for workmen injured on the job, and set up the Ontario Municipal Board.

On the south lawn is a recently erected memorial to police officers killed in the line of duty. They deserve something less maudlin.

DOWNTOWN: EAST

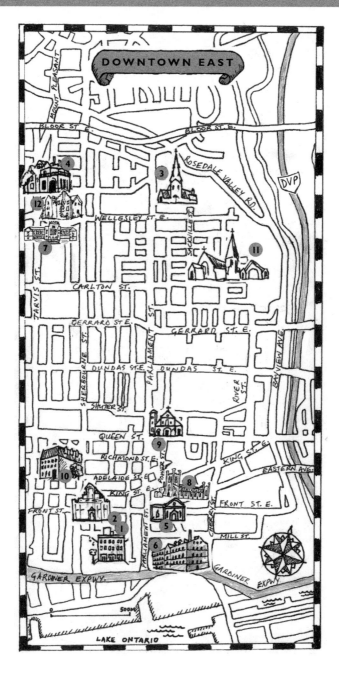

DOWNTOWN EAST

BERKELEY CASTLE
(A. J. DIAMOND, DONALD SCHMITT AND COMPANY)

2 Berkeley Street

Joseph Simpson opened a knitting business on this site near Front and Parliament Streets in 1874. It prospered and expanded, enabling Simpson to add new structures over the next few decades. By the middle of the twentieth century, these buildings had fallen into decline like the whole area south of Front Street, which consisted of derelict industrial buildings, auto-wrecking yards, open storage areas for coal, and shipping yards.

The big change came in 1973 when City Council hit on the innovative idea that this area held great potential for a new residential community. The City assembled most of the land between Yonge and Parliament and south from Front Street to the railway embankment. It then introduced a grid road system similar to that in the rest of the city, divided the land into building parcels, and awarded different social and private housing companies the right to construct a mixture of townhouses, apartments, and condominiums, interspersed with corner stores and other uses. The St. Lawrence Neighbourhood, as the new community is called, is now home to more than ten thousand residents, and the cohesive element is the linear park running along the Esplanade. The creation of the St. Lawrence community was one of the formative events of the 1970s in Toronto; it showed the attractiveness of living very close to the downtown and the positive role City Council could play in encouraging the construction of affordable housing.

The first structures in the new neighbourhood were started in 1975 at Jarvis and the Esplanade. As the development proceeded in an easterly course, Jack Diamond, a prominent Toronto architect, purchased the run-down industrial complex Simpson had spawned—and that the City had not acquired—and renamed it, perhaps whimsically,

Berkeley Castle Courtyard

A typical floor at Berkeley Castle.

Berkeley Castle. It became the office for his firm, A. J. Diamond, Donald Schmitt and Company. That firm and previous ones Diamond has been associated with are responsible for designing the Central YMCA on Grosvenor Street, the Hydro Block residential structures near Baldwin and Beverley, the Dundas–Sherbourne housing complex on the east side of Sherbourne, north of Dundas (City Council's first affordable housing project in the 1970s), and the Jerusalem City Hall.

Diamond was probably the first person in Toronto to take an old industrial building (the Eclipse Whitewear building at the northeast corner of King and John Streets) and convert it to attractive loft-type offices. He did the same with Berkeley Castle, and many others have followed his lead. This 1981 renovation has integrated the buildings into a single entity, while preserving the individual character of each structure for uses such as offices, showrooms, a retail shop, and of course the architectural office. A pleasant interior grassed courtyard has been created between several structures. This rehabilitation has been recognized with a national heritage award.

Across Berkeley Street and unmarked, although it can be seen behind a chain-link fence immediately to the west of a carwash on the south side of Front Street, is the site of the first Parliament buildings in Upper Canada. Built in 1797, they were burned to the ground by American troops who invaded the Town of York in the War of 1812. An archaeological dig undertaken in 2001 by the local group Citizens for the Old Town and funded largely by the City of Toronto has recently uncovered the evidence of the former Parliament buildings, including remnants of burnt wood, handmade nails, and fragments of dishware. The dig also uncovered artifacts from buildings that occupied the site at later dates, one being the second Parliament buildings—also destroyed by fire, this time accidentally—and Toronto's third jail, which was closed when the Don Jail opened in 1864. Sad to say, no level of government has yet been willing to recognize the importance of this heritage site by acquiring or protecting the property, even though the current owner wishes to construct a new building over the archaeological remains. The best governments have been willing to do is to erect a plaque 150 feet southeast of Berkeley Castle, indicating that the former Parliament buildings were somewhere in the vicinity—as one can perceive by the very name Parliament Street. It's shameful that public bodies are so chary of honouring the past.

Lieutenant-Governor John Graves Simcoe gave the order to build the first Parliament buildings in late 1795, but construction did not begin until 1797. The structure was to have comprised a central section and two wings, but the cost was deemed excessive, so the central section was not built. Thus the Parliament buildings consisted of two brick buildings, each about twenty-four feet by forty feet, some seventy-five feet apart. To the immediate east of each building was a smaller structure used for committee meetings. The Legislative Council met in one building, which also was used as a court, and the Legislative Assembly met in the other, which also served as an Anglican church.

When the American troops set fire to the buildings in 1813, the brick walls survived, and the structures were rebuilt to house British troops. Parliament met in several other locations until the second Parliament buildings were erected in 1819 on the same site. They burned down in 1824.

CANADIAN OPERA COMPANY
(JOEY AND TOBY TANENBAUM OPERA CENTRE)

227 Front Street East

Many large factories were located south of King Street, between Sherbourne Street and the Don River, during the latter half of the nineteenth century, and this structure, erected in 1885 and renovated in the past two decades as the administrative home of the Canadian Opera Company, shows how magnificent these buildings were.

In the 1860s, there was a strong demand in Toronto for gas to light homes and offices and to power industry. Coal was burned to produce gas, which was then distributed in pipes throughout the city. Consumers Gas Company began to thrive in this period, and it erected numerous buildings, including this one, built in 1889. A comparable structure still stands at the northeast corner of Front and Parliament Streets.

Converting coal to gas created considerable toxic waste, which often simply stayed in and around the building. The environmental damage can be rectified (as it has been here), but the expense of doing so accounts for why so much of the land east of Parliament Street lies derelict and empty—the gas plants have been demolished, but the toxins remain.

Once natural gas began to be piped into Toronto in the early 1950s—first from southwestern Ontario, then from Alberta—Consumers stopped manufacturing gas from coal. This particular building moved out of Consumers control in the 1930s when it was purchased by Dalton's, a food company famous in Canada for maraschino cherries. It was bought by the Canadian Opera Company in 1985.

From the exterior, the structure is large and lofty, with brick pillars and artificial window frames lessening the immense scale of the building. The eastern facade contains elements very similar in form to an Italian Renaissance basilica (compare it, for instance, with the similar form of St. Paul's church on Power Street) with fancy brickwork, arches, and stone caps on the piers. Inside, the building was originally one large space. There is some thought that the clerestory was designed so that if there was an explosion inside, the roof would blow off but the walls would remain intact.

The COC—viewed here looking westward along Front Street—makes its present home in what was once a Consumers Gas building.

With financial help from the local philanthropists Joey and Toby Tanenbaum, this building and the adjoining five-storey one to the west (originally a woollen mill, designed by E. J. Lennox, architect of the Old City Hall, and built in 1882) have been recently restored for offices, rehearsal space, workshops for the construction of scenery and other stage props, and storage space for wigs, costumes and archival material documenting musical performances in Toronto for over a hundred years.

CHAPEL OF ST. JAMES-THE-LESS

635 Parliament Street

This remarkable building was designed in 1860 by the architects **Cumberland & Storm**, designers of so many buildings of note in the city, including **University College**, and the centre section of **Osgoode Hall**

Frederic W. Cumberland had recently travelled to England, where he was refreshed by the ideas of John Ruskin, the influential critic and author. According to the writer John Bentley Mays, he was "ravished by a newfound love of the British Middle Ages." Thus, this chapel is Gothic in style, as Ruskin would have wished, with a very heavy bell tower, a steeply pitched roof that on its north side almost touches the ground, and wide masonry walls pierced by small arched windows through which shafts of light reach into the dark interior in a most dramatic fashion. The honey-hued walls and the closeness of the sloping roof give the interior a very warm and secure sense appropriate for those in the midst of the grieving process.

The basement was originally designed to hold the dead, awaiting burial services. Anglicans had preferred full burial to cremation for many centuries, even though unsanitary implications had been raised about burial in Victorian times. The debate about whether cremation would be acceptable for an Anglican was finally resolved in 1944 when the Archbishop of Canterbury, William Temple, on the point of death, indicated he wished to be cremated. He was, and the practice was deemed acceptable for Anglicans. The crematorium was installed here three years later. It is now a crematorium of choice for the local Sikh community, undoubtedly because of the chapel's atmosphere.

The name of the chapel refers to the larger St. James' Cathedral at King and Church Streets, and a longer story. In the 1830s, the burial ground around St. James' Cathedral became crowded: the cholera epidemic in 1834 killed five hundred people, or 10 per cent of the city's population, and the popular press blamed the escalation of the epidemic in part on the naturally swampy condition

The Austin tomb, resting place of James Austin. Born in Ireland, Austin started out as a grocer but moved into finance, founding the Dominion Bank and presiding over the Consumers Gas Company.

of the St. James' Cathedral cemetery. Cathedral officials looked beyond the city limits for a new burial ground—that was the Victorian approach to locating cemeteries—and secured this site on the east side of Parliament. After unexplained delays of almost a decade, the city surveyor, John Howard (who designed the original Mental Asylum at 999 Queen Street West, and later sold to the City the land that now makes up High Park) laid out the cemetery with a series of streets named after saints. With a burial ground so remote from the cathedral, it was then decided to place a chapel here—hence the name St. James-the-Less.

The cemetery contains some remarkable tombs, including the 1865 Austin family's—looking like a small house from Renaissance Italy—and the Gzowski tomb. Sir Casimir Gzowski was the son of a Polish

Inside the chapel.

count, and he made his fortune constructing the Grand Trunk Railway between Montreal Toronto, and the port of Sarnia, and also the large rolling mills that supplied the needed tracks, spikes, and bridges for the rail system. The 1861 Gzowski tomb was also designed by Cumberland but with an Egyptian theme. Cumberland himself is buried in this cemetery, as is the famous Toronto historian Dr. Henry Scadding.

CHESTER MASSEY HOUSE

519 Jarvis Street

It's hard to believe that Jarvis Street was once the preeminent location of the social and financial elite of Toronto, and referred to as "Millionaires' Row." In the intervening one hundred years the roadway has been widened to become an unpleasant, crowded traffic artery, and many of the stately mansions have been demolished to make way for apartment buildings and other structures of lesser interest.

But the two Massey houses on the east side of Jarvis, north of Wellesley, remain. The southern house, 515, was built in 1868 for the industrialist William McMaster but was later purchased by Hart Massey and renovated for his purposes. Today it serves as a restaurant. The house to the north, 519, was designed in the 1880s specifically for Charles Massey, and was the boyhood home of Vincent Massey, who

A view of the porte cochère.

played a large role in Canadian cultural life and became the country's first native-born governor general.

Number 519 was designed by the architect E. J. Lennox, responsible for the Old City Hall, Casa Loma, and other notable buildings in the city. He created it in the Queen Anne Style, that is, with many turrets, gables, complicated claddings, and other elements to make it picturesque. Numerous additions and changes have been made since Lennox's day. The sandstone porte cochère, with its carvings, was an addition early in the twentieth century (by Sproatt & Rolph, who designed Hart House) to accommodate the automobiles owned by Chester Massey, a subsequent occupant.

Inside is an impressive dining room by Lennox. Sproatt & Rolph designed the hallway around the stairs and the picture gallery in an

The interior as it was in 1909 (CITS 1244-306).

Arts and Crafts style, which emphasizes rustic and simple materials and design. The Gallery contains a Gustav Hahn mural. (Hahn was a well-known Toronto artist in the first half of the twentieth century, and Hahn Place in the St. Lawrence neighbourhood is named after him.) The picture gallery has its own skylight, apparently to enhance the paintings by Dutch masters, which Chester collected.

Several years ago, the provincial government, which owned both 515 and 519 Jarvis, offered the properties for sale and what appeared to be certain destruction. Cityscape Development Corporation, a company with a strong record of sensitively renovating historical properties, submitted an offer, only to find that the government was selling the property to the client of one of its main lobbyist friends, at a price lower than Cityscape had offered. Fortunately, those political plans were scotched by the court, and Cityscape gained ownership of the two sites and several at the rear. Cityscape is now in the process of restoring this house (restoration of the other will follow)—hopefully finding for each house a single user, such as a government embassy—and creating condominiums between and behind them in a complementary scale and style.

ENOCH TURNER SCHOOLHOUSE

106 Trinity Street

Outside Toronto's oldest school.

In the early 1800s, educating children in Toronto cost money, money that many poor families simply did not have. The problem was aggravated in this neighbourhood, which was home to many recent impecunious immigrants from Ireland.

In 1840 several local businessmen, including Enoch Turner, Joseph Shuter (whose name graces Shuter Street), and William Gooderham (of the Gooderham and Worts distillery), decided a new church and school were needed in the area. Construction of the church, Little Trinity, began in 1843 to designs by Henry Bowyer Lane, and was completed early the next year. But the funds were not available for the school, so the plans for it were shelved.

In 1848 Turner decided to proceed with the new school, providing his own funds. By then, the education situation had changed. The provincial government had passed legislation in 1847 stating that schooling should be provided at public cost, to be shared equally between the provincial and municipal governments. Toronto City Council refused to pay its share, and the province revoked its own contribution (struggles over financing and jurisdiction of education have a long history in Ontario), so that the fifteen public (or "common") schools in Toronto were closed from June 1848 to June 1849 until the contretemps was resolved. In January 1849, during this stalemate, Turner's schoolhouse opened for the children of Little Trinity Church. The school continued to operate here for a decade, with about a hundred children attending daily, taught by two teachers. In 1859 the children were moved to a new school, Palace Street School at the corner of Front (then called Palace) and Cherry. The old Palace Street School still stands—attached to the south end of the Canary Restaurant.

The facade of the school building, the oldest in the city, is modest, in traditional red and yellow brick with plain Gothic windows to either side of the door. The single classroom inside has been restored to its original purpose for the edification of today's children and is furnished with period desks and slates. A display case in the hallway offers artifacts from the school's early days—dolls, puzzles, games. Behind the classroom is West Hall, with a vaulted roof supported by handsome wooden beams, designed by Gundry & Langley. This was added in 1869, after Little Trinity Church had taken the site over for Sunday school purposes and more space was needed. This rear section now functions as a place for meetings and social gatherings.

By all accounts Enoch Turner was a consistent philanthropist. He was born in Straffordshire, England, in 1790, and came to York in 1830. He established a brewery on Taddle Creek, near Palace and Parliament Streets, but a serious fire in 1832 caused it great damage. The York Circus held a benefit for Turner, and he quickly returned to the brewing business. He was also successful in real estate, which gave him the means to provide funds to Little Trinity Church, and he was the largest benefactor of a fund establishing Trinity College in the 1850s. He had no children from either of his two marriages but was known to his extended family as a kind man, giving his horses beer after a particularly hard day. In 1855 he built a fine home at 245 Sherbourne Street—it still stands—and he lived there until his death in 1866.

Trinity Street feels much as it did in 1840s, when the school and Little Trinity Church abutting to the north were built. The houses on the east side of the street have stood since the nineteenth century, as have the buildings on the north side of King Street. This relatively neglected part of the city awaits renovation, which may be hastened by the new plans for the Gooderham and Worts project to the south.

The classroom, still furnished in the modest style befitting this mid-nineteenth-century schoolhouse.

GOODERHAM AND WORTS

🚪 55 Mill Street

Gooderham and Worts was a partnership of James Worts and his brother-in-law William Gooderham, two Englishmen who had come to York in the early 1830s. Their grist mill was first powered by a windmill located at the foot of Parliament Street. (A half-size copy was erected before the construction of the Gardiner Expressway in the 1960s but was demolished because it was in the way. It is now recalled in the name of the Windmill Housing Co-op, just south of Berkeley Castle.)

This five-storey limestone building was used during the First World War to manufacture Acetone, used in the production of explosives.

The three condominium towers immediately surrounding the Gooderham and Worts complex were created by Michel Labbé's company, Options for Homes. Purchasers are required to take a small second mortgage, the funds from which are used to allow some units to be marketed at even more modest prices so there is a real income mix within these buildings. This socially responsive model has proven attractive to many purchasers.

The Pure Spirits building.

The small operation prospered and expanded to include distilling, eventually serving markets across Canada, the United States, and the Commonwealth, leading to the construction of what is now this national historic site, comprising a forty-seven-building complex constructed from the late 1850s onward.

The most remarkable building of the group is the five-storey limestone one on the west side of Trinity Street, close to the railway lines. The stone was imported from Kingston, and the walls of the foundation are more than a yard thick. The style is simple, interrupted only by a slightly raised course at the sill level for each floor. The windows are plain and unframed. Grain was raised by elevator from the railway cars and stored in the upper floors of the building. The grindstones were on the lower floors at the east end of the building, and the whisky distillery was at the west end.

Many buildings were added over the years, including the Mill Street office building topped with the cupola lantern, and the Pure Spirits building, which, with its vast quantities of glass and clean straight lines, appears exceedingly modern. The many plain brick structures around the site, with their timber racks and roofs, were used for the aging of alcohol—apparently the separate structures limited the danger of fire damage. Linkages between them is accomplished, where necessary, with overhead bridges for pipes. The streets between the buildings remain paved in brick, as they were in the nineteenth century, providing an environment that many movie directors have found irresistible.

Overhead bridges were used to house pipes that connected some buildings in the complex. The Pure Spirits building is on the left.

The heritage designation of the complex has raised many concerns for developers interested in buying the property, but it was considered a bonus for Cityscape Development Corporation, which purchased it in late 2001. Cityscape has made a business of respecting and restoring historic properties (such as the Stewart Building at 135 College Street, or the Massey mansions on Jarvis Street north of Wellesley), and plans to do the same here. The intention is to use this complex as a focus for the arts, with artists' studios, exhibition and sales spaces, and performance spaces, all fitting into the buildings as they are and the areas between them. The hope is that this can be a cultural marketplace with the same kind of ambience as Granville Island in Vancouver, which people see as a cultural destination.

JARVIS COLLEGIATE

🏛 495 Jarvis Street

Jarvis Collegiate today

Toronto has a marvellous array of high schools that seem to have been built as English castles. "Collegiate Gothic" is the name stuck to them, but Central Tech (at Bathurst and Harbord Streets) is more Tudor than Gothic, as is Jarvis Collegiate.** Jarvis has large windows on all three floors that march down the street, and above are battlements and parapets on the roofline. The building's broad steps convey an air of solemnity that continues through the front doors to the grey marble walls of the lobby. The inside hall is wide and the ceiling proportionately high.

Jarvis Collegiate was named after the street, in turn named after the Jarvis family of the ruling Family Compact in the early nineteenth century. Samuel Jarvis, son of William, the paterfamilias, took credit for leading the crew of hooligans who broke into the print shop of

William Lyon Mackenzie in 1826 and carried off the type that was unceremoniously thrown into the Toronto Bay. He also killed his former friend John Ridout in a duel in 1817, although he was acquitted of murder at trial.

Inside the building, the auditorium is particularly interesting. It is lined with almost a dozen panels designed by George Reid, who also did the paintings above the interior arches of Old City

Samuel Peters Jarvis (1792–1857) was a powerful member of government and by most accounts a rogue. His colourful reputation suffered badly in 1845, when he was dismissed from his post as superintendent of Indian Affairs for misappropriation of public funds to the tune of £4,000.

William Jarvis came to York from Niagara in 1798 and built his first home at the corner of Sherbourne and Adelaide Streets. He was the provincial secretary, a significant post that made him part of what William Lyon Mackenzie called the Family Compact, the group of elites that was the de facto government in Upper Canada until just after the rebellion of 1837. William's son Samuel strengthened the Family Compact connection by marrying into the family of William Powell, a chief justice in Upper Canada. Samuel's home, Hazelburn, was located on the street bearing the family name. A non-profit housing co-operative, built in the 1980s on Jarvis Street just north of Shuter Street, has taken the name Hazelburn as its own.

Hall's main entrance. These panels sprang from the experience of the Great War, 1914–18, which had a significant impact on Toronto schools. For instance, more than two hundred students, teachers, and graduates of Harbord Collegiate enlisted in the Great War, and seventy-five did not return. The grief at the school was significant, so a memorial was commissioned by former students—a bronze statue by George Hill, which now stands in front of that school. Similarly, Malvern Collegiate in the east end commissioned a sculpture by Emanuel Hahn and Central Tech one by Alfred Howell. When Jarvis Collegiate opened in 1924, the idea of memorial art was not far from officials' minds.

Reid, then principal of the Ontario College of Art, was approached, and he proposed a series of paintings. Flanking the stage would be panels about the war titled *Patriotism* and *Sacrifice*, while around the room would be pictures showing explorers of Canada such as John Cabot and Alexander Mackenzie, the Hudson's Bay Company, and so forth. Natives were pictured in noble poses. Reid created the panels over the next two decades and his widow, Mary Wrinch, completed a panel as late as 1949, showing a seascape during the Second World War.

This extraordinary piece of art is but one of many found in Toronto schools—stained-glass windows in Danforth Tech, a Frances Loring carving at Western Tech, and many other fine works that sadly are easily passed over.

The Discoverers, 1500 to 1610, the third of eleven George Reid murals that grace the auditorium.

LITTLE TRINITY CHURCH

425 King Street East

The front doorway, with a Gothic arch surrounded by a more elegant stone wishbone, announces the date of the structure—1843—on either side of the door. St. James' Cathedral at King and

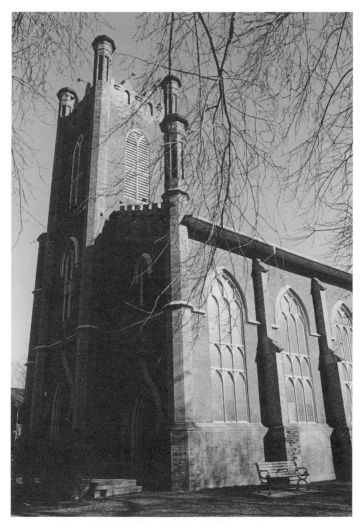

Church Streets burned down in 1849. Little Trinity became the oldest church of any faith in the city.

The style is Gothic but plain, with six large, pointed, multi-paned windows on either side of the structure. The architect was Henry Bowyer Lane, designer of the Church of the Holy Trinity a few years later, and one can see here at the corners of the building the octagonal columns that later became the more interesting turrets on either side of the main door at Holy Trinity. The bell tower is crowned with four blunt octagonal turrets, one at each corner, and the bell can still be heard every week, calling congregants to worship. Inside, the furnishings date back to the 1840s—the pulpit, the Communion table, the baptistery, and the pews. The simplicity of the building had much to do with the fact that this was a poor Irish working-class community, also served by St. Paul's Basilica, the Roman Catholic church three blocks to the north.

Funds for construction came from William Gooderham, owner of the distillery to the south and others. The first rector of the church, Rev. William Ripley, served without remuneration, and according to the architectural historian Eric Arthur, to ensure that the meagre church budget was not exceeded, "the twenty-four-burner gaselier used to be turned low during the sermon, putting the congregation 'into the hazy mystery of semi-darkness, a condition very favourable for napping or little social amenities.'" A fire in 1889 destroyed the addition of a chancel and choir, and renovations returned the structure to Lane's original design.

The building immediately to the west was the original rectory, by Cumberland & Storm, but it now seems almost entirely swallowed by ramps, and the structures just a bit farther west (now boarded up) date from the same period. The church has been unable to find a buyer interested in restoration. Perhaps another condominium block may be built like that on the corner property, "The Derby," named after the tavern that existed on this site for almost 140 years, until the early 1980s.

ST. PAUL'S BASILICA

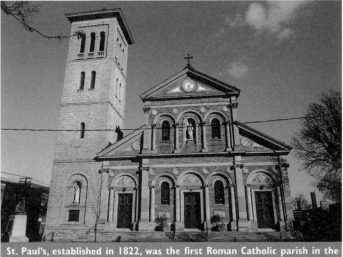

83 Power Street

With the influx of Irish immigrants in the early nineteenth century, Roman Catholic authorities established a parish in Toronto. St. Paul's was its first church. It grew in size and influence, and the current building, St. Paul's Basilica, was built during the 1880s to replace earlier structures. The architect was (of course) an Irish immigrant, Joseph Connolly, who had been trained in Dublin. Another example of his work in Toronto is the soaring Gothic marvel St. Mary's Roman Catholic Church on Bathurst Street at Adelaide.

St. Paul's is an entirely different kind of building, one that is a rarity in Toronto. Its model is Santa Maria Novella in Florence, or perhaps the basilica St. Paul's Outside the Walls, in Rome. It is a rational Italian Renaissance–style building with a central nave structure twice as high as the sections over the aisles and a sturdy tower set to one side. Rather than any stress of Gothic verticality, this building features the rounded arch, which lifts toward heaven only to return to earth where humans are. A sense of calmness and rationality abounds.

The architectural historian Eric Arthur writes that the interior is

St. Paul's, established in 1822, was the first Roman Catholic parish in the present Archdiocese of Toronto.

"quite the most beautiful in Toronto," and he's not far off the mark. It is white and full of light from the clerestory windows, with rounded arches that lend solidity and serenity. There are no shadows, nothing unknown or unknowable. Paintings and sculptures in the aisles focus on the life and death of Christ, paintings on the ceiling on St. Paul. The acoustics are outstanding, a perfect complement to the oldest wooden organ in Toronto, which is housed here.

For many years the House of Providence stood immediately to the south of St. Paul's. It was a four-storey French-château-like structure built in the 1850s to serve the poor, the sick, the old, and the abandoned, which it did with great distinction. Unfortunately, this building was demolished in the 1950s to make way for the easterly extension of Richmond Street so that it could be paired with Adelaide to become the on and off ramps for the Don Valley Parkway. Today these roads are an intrusion into the neighbourhood, making the area south of the Basilica feel much like a wasteland.

On August 26, 1999, Pope John Paul II designated St. Paul's a Minor Basilica— the first and only one in the city. To receive such a title, a church must be deemed a centre of liturgical worship and pastoral work in the archdiocese and of particular historical or other significance.

During the 1960s the basement of St. Paul's was the location of meetings that led to significant change in city politics. City Council intended to demolish the Trefann Court community between Parliament and River Streets north of Queen and then rebuild it in a modern style, as an urban renewal project. (The name came from Trefann Street, immediately north of the church.) Local residents and business people argued forcefully that rather than being destroyed, the neighbourhood should be improved, and residents should be involved in planning for the rehabilitation of houses and businesses. After five years of filing briefs, attending meetings, and organizing demonstrations, residents wore the politicians down enough that in 1971 City Council relented. It abandoned the plan of expropriation and agreed that residents could be members of a working committee to create a plan to preserve and strengthen the Trefann area. That led to the City's comprehensive (and highly lauded) strategy to preserve and enhance neighbourhoods and to engage residents in planning—"citizen participation," as it was tagged.

The ceiling is decorated with outstanding paintings depicting events from the apostle Paul's life.

TORONTO'S FIRST POST OFFICE

260 Adelaide Street East

The structure known as Toronto's first post office in fact was the fourth post office for the Town of York and the earliest and only remaining one in the city when Toronto officially came into being in 1834. It was built in the early 1830s and served the population of nine thousand from 1833 to 1839. It has been restored in the past twenty years through private initiatives to again serve as an active post office, starting in December 15, 1983—

the 150th anniversary of the first day it opened for business.

The three-and-a-half-storey exterior is simple red brick, with plain windows and a mansard roof. It was built by James Scott Howard, postmaster of York, not only to serve as a post office but also to house his family. During the 1837 Rebellion, the postmaster was alleged to have sympathized with the rebels and was dismissed. The post office then moved to another location, Howard was forced to rent out the building, and it has had many different functions since that time. It was used by nearby De La Salle College beginning in 1873, by the Catholic Separate School Board until 1916, was sold to Christie, Brown and Company, whose main bakery (now part of George Brown College) was across the street, and then to United Farmers Co-operative, who used it from 1925 on as a cold storage facility for butter and eggs. It fell into decline in the 1960s and was almost levelled in a fire in 1978. The present owners rescued the building in 1982.

The first floor has been refurbished to duplicate a post office of the 1830s. Visitors are encouraged to pick up a quill pen to write a letter, then seal it with wax, and post it to a friend. The topographical model of the city as it was in 1837 is of considerable help in understanding how the town then functioned.

The block where the post office is situated is one of the most historically significant in Toronto. Immediately east was the home of Justice William Campbell, built in the 1820s. (To avoid demolition in 1971, this structure was moved to the corner of University and Queen Streets.) To the west is the original De La Salle College, built in 1873, and beside it (at 252) is the Bank of Upper Canada, built in 1826 and, like the post office, owned and rehabilitated largely through private initiative. (It does seem strange that two very important buildings in Toronto's history are not under public control but rely on private beneficiaries to survive.) The bank played an important role in Toronto's growth. Gold was stored in the basement vault, so this was the building William Lyon Mackenzie and other rebels thought of as they marched down Yonge Street in December 1837.

During colonial days, the British government ran postal facilities in Canada directly from England. As a leading reformer, William Lyon Mackenzie vociferously complained about the lack of local control, claiming the British authorities used the postal service primarily to generate revenue rather than to facilitate the exchange of letters and information. Mackenzie gave many examples, showing that it was faster and less expensive to send mail to Britain using the American post office. It was not until 1851, fourteen years after the Rebellion, that Britain allowed Canada to run its own postal services.

It is a pity that Adelaide Street is one-way, flooded with cars racing by at a ferocious speed. Larger front yards, wider sidewalks, and calmer traffic patterns would do wonders for these very important Toronto buildings, as well as for the citizens that pass by, unaware.

This functioning post office also serves as a publicly funded museum.

TORONTO NECROPOLIS CEMETERY

200 Winchester Street

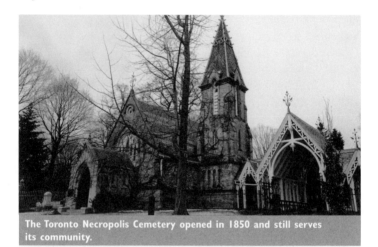

The Toronto Necropolis Cemetery opened in 1850 and still serves its community.

Т he Necropolis—the Greek term for "the City of the Dead"—was established in the mid-nineteenth century to provide burial space on a non-denominational basis when Potter's Field, the city's general burying ground in Yorkville, was becoming overcrowded.

The remarkable Victorian Gothic buildings at its entrance were designed in the 1870s by Henry Langley, architect of the towers of the three large churches downtown. The porte cochère has delicate wooden tracery under the eaves and light spindly columns supporting the roof. The chapel and crematorium on the left feel almost tiny—the interior holds hardly more than five dozen people—but is finely executed. The adjoining tower also seems miniaturized and is graced with a charming copper spire. The lodge where the cemetery's caretaker and administrative staff have their offices is residential in character. Linking these structures stylistically is the patterned decoration on the steeply sloping slate roofs. This is the finest entryway to a cemetery in the city, inviting and almost celebratory. There's nothing here about the gloom of death.

William Lyon Mackenzie and many members of his family are buried in this cemetery. (Plot O-94. From the entrance, walk straight ahead, turn right at the end of the path, and walk seventy-five paces to the large Celtic cross memorial on the left.) The remains of Peter Matthews and Samuel Lount, the two rebels hanged in 1838 for their part in the Rebellion, were moved to this site toward the end of the nineteenth century and a memorial erected consisting of a tragically broken column. (Plot C-19. It is located just east of Sumach Street.) Other notables buried here are George Brown, a father of Confederation, publisher of *The Globe*, and Reform politician (Plot E-85); Toronto's world-famous rower Ned Hanlan, after whom one of the islands in Toronto Bay is named (Plot C-40); John Ross Robertson, founder of the influential newspaper the *Evening Telegram* in 1876 (Plot O-221); and Canada's first native-born black surgeon, Anderson Ruffin Abbot (Plot VNG-75). While it is pleasant to walk on the pathways here, more people would do so if they realized there are many discoveries to make along the way, and to that end a map identifying important plots would be helpful. Burial plots are still available.

In the mid-1860s it was thought this eighteen-acre site might be too small, and the trustees of the Necropolis purchased more land on the south side of Winchester Street. Residents of the surrounding community objected to the expansion, and the trustees decided instead to purchase what is now Mount Pleasant Cemetery. The resulting extra parcel of land was later acquired by the city and for much of the twentieth century was the Riverdale Zoo, until construction of the Metro Zoo in the 1970s. When the zoo here closed, residents wanted some facility with animals to remain on the site, so the City established Riverdale Farm with a complement of pigs, cows, chickens, and other farmyard animals, to the delight of many children and neighbours, who greet the morning in the city at the crowing of a rooster. It has been said that Toronto has the only urban 4H Club (the popular club for kids living on farms) in Canada.

Inside the chapel.

WELLESLEY PLACE, 2 AND 4

One can hardly think of a less becoming place to have a home than on the laneway known as Wellesley Place. It was not always so. Before the large red-brick Wellesley Hospital, now closed and awaiting demolition, was built, the home of the businessman Benjamin Homer Dixon—whose sister Harriette Boulton was by the fortune of marriage living in the Grange—occupied a large parcel of land on the other side of Wellesley Place, giving these houses a pleasant view to the east.

Number 2 Wellesley Place was the home of the industrialist Rupert Simpson, son of the owner of the city's first knitting mill, located on the property now occupied by Berkeley Castle. The house was designed by Charles Gibson (originally from Quebec City but trained in New York via England) in 1899 in the Richardson Romanesque mode with sturdy round arches, much red brick and sandstone, and considerable carving and terra-cotta decoration. The front entrance is exceptionally impressive with its heavy stone staircase, solid decorated columns, and roomy porch. There is a wealth of detail to admire on the facade, an oriel window on the north, and a stepped gable on the south.

Inside, the front rooms of the house are unaltered, still dressed with fine wood and plaster mouldings. The drawing room ceiling moulding with small lights is not to be missed. In the rear yard, the stable, now being renovated, served several decades ago as a studio for the artist Ken Danby.

Number 4 Wellesley Place is a much more modest building, in a design often seen in Ontario: a door to one side, an Italianate bay window to the other, and fancy wood trim at the roofline. The builder went to considerable trouble to add value to this structure by using quoins at the corners as well as arching the windows on the second floor. The semicircular transom over the main door is in handsome stained glass. In recent years this building has served as the White Light Hospice and Respite Care Centre.

Like the buildings directly to the west, these structures have been recently purchased from the provincial government by Cityscape Development Corporation, which plans to build infill housing behind, then renovate and find appropriate uses for these two houses, such as a bed-and-breakfast operation.

The Wellesley Hospital site across the street is owned by a hospital foundation, and the former Princess Margaret Hospital immediately to the north by the provincial government. City officials have been working to persuade a reluctant province to replace these large, ungainly, and unusable structures with a redevelopment that includes housing for a range of incomes, a small health care centre, and a community facility. If such a plan comes to pass, it should be a significant benefit to the two houses that now feel a bit abandoned on Wellesley Place.

Doors Open participants at 2 Wellesley Place.

DOWNTOWN: WEST

ANSHEI MINSK SYNAGOGUE

10 St. Andrew Street

In the early years of the twentieth century, many immigrants to Toronto found their first homes in the relative squalor of the Ward, the area north of Queen Street between Bay and University.

With the advent of the Great War in 1914, the number of Jews from Eastern Europe coming to Canada increased considerably. The swelling numbers and the pressures for redevelopment meant that immigrants had to seek out other places to live, so many in the Jewish community moved west near Spadina Avenue. East of Spadina, houses were larger and more expensive, only affordable to better-off families. A few signs of the area's once-vibrant Jewish life still exist there. The window of John's Italian Café at 27 Baldwin shows the Hebrew lettering from the original poultry shop, and a synagogue remains on Henry Street at Cecil, although it is now used by a Russian Orthodox congregation.

But poverty more often forced the Jewish community into the smaller houses on the west side of Spadina. An outdoor market was quickly established there, said to feel more European than one might find in New York City. It is thought that in the 1920s some thirty synagogues were located west of Spadina in the area known as Kensington Market.

The Anshei Minsk Synagogue is one of the few still standing in downtown Toronto and is a fine example of the Eastern European style of the time. The central portion of the building is embraced by two slightly protruding arms, modestly decorated with arches and tall windows—a form differing only in matters of detail from the Kiever Shul Synagogue at Denison Square and Bellevue Avenue, several blocks to the west, or with the Henry Street building. The steps leading up to the main entrance separate the place of worship from day-to-day street life. Inside are stained-glass windows and an ornate chandelier, but the interior character is best expressed by the simple wooden floors: in spite of the musical instruments on the walls, this is a no-nonsense place of worship.

During the 1950s, the Jewish community moved north on Bathurst Street near Eglinton Avenue, making room for new immigrants to begin their Canadian lives in Kensington. In the latter half of the twentieth century, Kensington has provided a new start to people from, among other places, Italy, the Caribbean, Portugal, China, Thailand, and Central America. As one can tell just by walking on the streets of Kensington, this is the most polyglot of neighbourhoods. After losing its local congregants, the Anshei Minsk Synagogue is managing to attract young people, particularly from the nearby university, and is undergoing a spiritual revitalization that hopefully will be soon reflected in the physical revitalization that the exterior of this structure so richly deserves.

Construction of the building began in 1922. When it was completed in 1930, the synagogue became one of approximately thirty synagogues located in the Spadina–Kensington Market area.

CAMPBELL HOUSE

160 Queen Street West

Wiilliam Campbell was born in Caithness, Scotland, in 1758, and after studying law for several years he joined the Highland Regiment as a soldier. He fought for the British in the American War of Independence and was taken prisoner, finally being released in 1783. He then came to Halifax, where he joined the navy, married Hannah Handley, a local woman, and went back to the study of law.

Campbell entered the world of business and was acclaimed to the Legislative Assembly in 1799, where he was noted for his political ability

and his principled outspokenness. His skills led to his appointment as attorney general for Cape Breton, but several years later he was dismissed for reasons that are not clear. His moral convictions may have been the cause, since when he went to England to appeal his dismissal, he earned appointment as a judge in Upper Canada.

He assumed this new position in 1811, and soon felt able to commission a house befitting his prominence and salary. In 1822 he had one built on Duke (now Adelaide) Street: a red-brick building with strong echoes of the Grange, built a few years earlier. Campbell's home looked down Frederick Street, with a view of the town's bay. It existed at this location for a century and a half, until 1972 when the owner decided to demolish it. Fortunately, after an approach by buyers, he agreed to sell it to the Advocates Society for $1, providing it was moved

from the site. The present location at Queen and University was secured, on land owned by Canada Life Assurance Company, on condition that the City waive the considerable property taxes.

The move took place in 1972 on Good Friday, one of the quietest days of the year. The building weighed some three hundred tons; lifting it in almost one piece (the porch and tail were removed) and placing it on a large dolly with wheels was a major engineering feat. It was bulky enough to require the temporary removal of overhead streetcar wires along the route, as well as several traffic lights, utility poles, and street lights, so the structure could lumber along on at a

On March 31, 1972, Campbell House was moved more than a mile from its original location—the longest journey in history of a building of this size. To accommodate its passage through downtown, eighty-two street lights were loosened and swung sideways, and some sixty-five manholes were shored up to guard against collapse under the weight of the great house.

speed of about ten feet a minute, surrounded by a crowds of curious onlookers. With stronger preservation legislation—municipalities are permitted to delay demolition of a structure for no more than 180 days, after which the owner can treat the building as rubbish—the building might have remained on Adelaide Street next to the city's oldest post office, from the 1830s, and just along the street from the former Bank of Upper Canada.

One example of Mr. Justice Campbell's strong sense of conviction and fairness occurred in 1826, when he was presiding at a case involving York's famous reformer, William Lyon Mackenzie. A group of young men—sons of the Family Compact, the elite that felt it had a right to make the important decisions in Upper Canada—had broken into Mackenzie's shop on Frederick Street and tossed his type into the harbour. Mackenzie sued for restitution. Campbell's friendship with many members of the Compact did not interfere with his judgment, which awarded Mackenzie enough to pay off his debts and begin republishing his newspaper, the Colonial Advocate.

The building is a good example of strong, plain, well-proportioned Georgian architecture. Five large windows punctuate the second floor, matched by four windows and the doorway at grade. The elliptical window in the pediment is matched by the semi-elliptical transom window over the main door. The porch, with four columns, is small but elegant. The Advocates Society maintains a museum in the basement (open to the public) and club quarters on the main floor.

While the building's new location makes it feel a bit like a fish out of water, it is again close to the courts, and the Legislature is just up the street. The fence surrounding the property has none of the elegance the building deserves, compared with the fencing of the Canada Life building to the north, or of Osgoode Hall down the street. Sadly, a sidewalk air vent near the southwest corner of the property is often occupied by the homeless.

Across Queen Street is a bank building with simple, strong pillars, pediment, and lovely copper carvings like a temple to Mithridates. One can imagine Mr. Justice Campbell being happy to look out of an upstairs window of his home's new location to see this building.

CANADA LIFE ASSURANCE COMPANY

330 University Avenue

A number of impressive Toronto buildings were begun in the late 1920s boom and completed in the barren, depressed early 1930s. This fine office structure designed by Sproatt & Rolph is an example.

It is described alternately as an example of the Beaux-Arts style—because of the very graceful stone decoration, the bronze around the

The Canada Life building, just completed (CTA 1244-3172).

Workmen laying the last stone of the building in 1929 (CTA 1244-116).

doors, the iron grille and fence work—or neo-classical—given the large Doric columns over the main entrance and the severe, symmetrical organization of the elements.

The architects went to great trouble to reduce the bulk of the building with four sections decreasing in size as they ascend. The first rises a single floor and defines the foundation, even though this is the level experienced at grade. The second section includes the columns, which create a kind of portico not accessible from the street. This central portion has narrow balconies that appear to provide abutting offices with immediate access to the open air of University Avenue. The third section of the building encompasses four storeys and appears to be the meatiest portion of the structure. At the top of this section the balconies are repeated. The upper part consists of a two-storey cap and a much thinner, tiered tower. On the very top of the building the weather beacon has for more than fifty years flashed predictions about temperature rising and falling and the likelihood of rain or snow.

A good view of this structure is from the boulevard down the centre of University Avenue. One's eye rises with the design, slowly and steadily to the top. The design states that this is a solid company, but not without grace, perhaps offering investors the assurance they need about the safety of their money with Canada Life. The decorative keystones over the main doors and windows and the disks in the stone coursing add notes of elegance.

The main door is large and the surrounding brass work exquisitely detailed. Before an equally glorious second set of doors, the visitor is caught for a moment in a warm grey-stoned interval with decorated stone domes. Then one enters a foyer with inlaid marble on the floor, warm stone walls all around, glistening black pillars, fine glass-and-brass lighting fixtures, and a ceiling decorated with gold disks. It is an exceptionally comfortable way to enter an important financial building, and it leads on to an equally impressive bank of elevators. One only wishes that contemporary buildings had such grace and style. The elevators rise seventeen storeys, and when first built they offered a view rivalled only by the Bank of Commerce at King and Bay Streets.

On leaving the building, note the war memorial in the middle of University Avenue, just slightly to the south of the main doors. It was designed by Walter Allward, the same sculptor responsible for the famous Vimy Ridge memorial for Canadians killed in the First World War, and the memorial to William Lyon Mackenzie to the west of the Legislative Buildings. While this one honours those killed in the Boer War in South Africa at the turn of the twentieth century, it was not built until 1936.

A block west of the main building is a pleasant-enough new office structure containing the Canada Life Environmental Room on the main floor. This room has a "breathing wall" of carefully selected plants and aquatic creatures that purify air in the building and restore oxygen to it. This is one of the new "natural system" techniques being used to address problems that too often in the past relied (often unsuccessfully) on mechanical means. The breathing wall has been in place for several years, and it is still being studied before it (hopefully) receives widespread application.

The Canada Life Environmental Room houses a variety of plants and aquatic creatures. Its key feature, a "breathing wall," purifies the recycled air.

CASA LOMA STABLES

328½ Walmer Road

In the first few years of the twentieth century, Albert Austin, whose family owned the house Spadina, decided to subdivide his golf course to its west and sell the land. Sir Henry Pellatt, one of the more high-profile businessmen in Toronto, purchased twenty-five of these lots and hired E. J. Lennox, architect of Old City Hall, to design him a grand new home. Lennox started with the stables on Walmer Road in 1906 and several years later built the extraordinary Casa Loma, with its towers, turrets, chimneys, and ninety-eight rooms.

A 1920 view of the stables.

Pellatt was not short of money or vision. In the 1880s he had been a successful stockbroker, and in the 1890s he acquired vast wealth by investing in the creation of electrical generation plants at Niagara Falls. He was a military man as well, his regiment being the Queen's Own Rifles, which he sponsored in the castle. When he came to instructing his architect, he was not about to shirk on money spent or the pomposity of the structures. For his part, Lennox himself never shied away from the flamboyant or the dramatic.

The entrance to the stables sets the scene. Large stone pillars support lavish decorative ironwork gates that open onto a gravelled courtyard. Just inside the fence, and closest to the street, is a tower (recently restored) with turrets and chimneys and a Dutch-style roof on the south side. The interior of the tower is almost inaccessible—a small door and behind it a very narrow circular staircase provide the only access to the six levels of the seventy-foot tower. Furniture and larger items can be moved in only through a ceiling drop in each floor, which permits them to be hoisted up. The tower serves primarily to impress the viewer—which it does in magnificent style—although its many levels, with their tiny windows, did find use as a barracks for the troops under Pellatt's command.

To the right of the courtyard is the doorway to the stables proper.

Surrounding the wooden doors (with their multi-paned, almost elliptical windows) are grey sandstone banded columns topped with gorgeously carved rearing horses. Between them is Pellatt's crest, and above them the red brick of the two-storey structure. The main foyer has walls of white glazed brick, with a delicate blue meander pattern just below the heavy wooden beams of the ceiling, and a floor of red and yellow tile in a herringbone pattern, so designed to ensure the horses would not slip. To the left are the stalls, in dark Spanish mahogany. At the head of each stall is a water container and a backboard of sky blue tile with the brass name plate of the horse.

Leading from the main doors is the carriage room, cathedral-like, with heavy exposed decorative wood beams, small windows under the eaves, and at the head of the room, a rose window. A pattern of yellow, maroon, and green bricks embellishes the basic white glazed brick. There are a dozen carriages, several of which belonged to Pellatt, and four sleighs. The sliding doors of the carriage room can be seen only from the inside of the room. The doors hanging in the entrance way are of more recent construction—they were made for use during filming of *X-Men* here. Leading off the foyer to the right is a wood-panelled tack room and a large tiled stall where horses could be washed.

The quality of the design and the cost of materials was so high (it is said the stables alone cost more than $250,000—an enormous sum then) that it is hard to believe this is a home for horses. Note that the lintel over every door and window is gently arched, adding much elegance to this space.

Again in the courtyard, the second entrance is linked to the stable by a portico, above which two dormer windows allow light and air into the second-floor area, probably used to bunk down Pellatt's troops. The second entrance is as grand as that leading to the stables. The statues on the banded columns are rearing lions, and crowding them are imperious-looking red-brick turrets with conical roofs. This was the garage. Sir Henry owned a car and had a chauffeur. The chauffeur's day room is just inside these doors and to the right, where his desk and a map of Southern Ontario, both from the First World War era, can still be seen. His living quarters are accessible by the small circular staircase directly inside the main garage doors.

Inside the doorway at the south end of the garage are stairs to the tunnel to Casa Loma. Pellatt wanted this tunnel to ease the walk by his staff and his troops between the castle and the stable. Past the stairway to the tunnel is a one-storey potting shed, extending to the south. The basement level of this structure contains the boiler that heats not only the stable area but Casa Loma itself. The potting shed's main floor is a simple large room with four doors on the east wall. Each door once led to its own small greenhouse: before demolition, these glass structures occupied what is now a lawn between the potting shed and Walmer Road. Just to the south of the potting shed is the two-

The stables played a unique role during the Second World War. In 1941, to the knowledge of almost no one until after the war, the Royal Navy began assembling here its newest and most secret weapon—sonar. The official name of the operation was Anti-Submarine Detection Investigation Committee (ASDIC), and the device it created could identify a German U-boat from a distance of five miles underwater. Twenty mechanics worked here, and the space was perfect, not only because of the high ceilings required to house the completed device, but also because who would have thought that the stables of Casa Loma could be the centre of such an important clandestine operation?

storey house known as the Hunting Lodge, designed as Pellatt's home until construction of Casa Loma was completed in 1911. The Hunting Lodge is owned by the City of Toronto and was leased until recently as a private residence. Discussions are now under way between West Toronto Kiwanis Club, which manages the stables and Casa Loma, and the City about the Club taking over this building so that it might be put to some use that brings it into the public realm.

The garage, part of the stables complex, in 1952. The two dormer windows on the steeply pitched roof belong to the chauffeur's living quarters.

CITY OF TORONTO ARCHIVES

255 Spadina Road

The first impression of the Archives building is that it is set too far back from the street. Buildings to the north are much closer and provide a definition of the street edge, but here there's too much lawn. This was not one of the design ideas of the architects, Zeidler Roberts, but a dictate of the former Metro Toronto Council, which commissioned the building in the early 1990s.

The setback has to do with Metro's unhappiness with a decision made more than twenty years previously. Throughout the 1960s, Metro Council believed that the way to solve Toronto's transportation problems was to build expressways from the burgeoning suburbs into the heart of the city. One favourite scheme was the Spadina Expressway, planned to run from Yorkdale Shopping-Centre south through neighbourhoods and ravines until it reached the Casa Loma steps, where it would blast through the escarpment and head south in a ditch on Spadina Avenue until it surfaced in the vicinity of College Street. This proposal was contentious, particularly among those living along the route of the expressway. Affected citizens took the matter to the provincial politicians, and in June 1971 Premier William Davis made the extraordinary decision to stop the expressway—now called W. R. Allen Road—at Eglinton Avenue. Metro Council never

accepted this decision and built the University–Spadina subway line in the ravine (rather than the more logical route down Bathurst Street) to preserve a right-of-way in the hope that the expressway decision would be reversed. The setback of the Archives building continues that dream by maintaining the widened right-of-way on Spadina Avenue.

The Archives' facade consists of red brick and horizontal bands of stone that arch around the windows. This design calls to mind many city buildings constructed in the early 1930s under the leadership of then Works Commissioner R. C. Harris (his name is attached to the large water filtration plant in the city's east end). That series was a response to the Depression and the need to create jobs, and they had a common form: yellow bricks, horizontal bands of stone, and Art Deco detailing. The bands of stone here are a nice post-modern touch, making a clear

The City of Toronto Archives was designed by Zeidler Roberts Partnership and opened in 1992. The records inside date back to the late 1700s.

The fight to stop the Spadina Expressway was one of the formative events in Toronto politics, showing that citizen pressure can achieve important results. Premier William Davis's words have become famous: "If we are building a transportation system to serve the automobile, the Spadina Expressway would be a good start. But if we are building a transportation system to serve the people, the Spadina Expressway is a good place to stop." To accomplish that, Davis gave the City of Toronto a three-foot-wide strip of land in the expressway's path just south of Eglinton Avenue, with the proviso that it can never be used for roadway purposes.

reference to the other public buildings. Variation in the Archives' facade is provided by recesses in the wall face under the windows.

A small tower and cupola mark the entrance. Inside, a two-storey atrium hosts exhibitions on local issues. The remainder of the structure serves archival and storage purposes—some visible through the glass wall. This is a high-tech facility, with the latest bells and whistles to protect archival material—air filtration, temperature controls, humidity monitors, and so forth, to respect the fragility of paper, photographs, maps, audiovisual material, computer records, and artifacts from as far back as the founding of the Town of York in 1793. Study space is available for students and scholars.

The residential development across the street—Castle Hill, in a neo-Georgian style reminiscent of Bath, England—is also set back in deference to the ghost of the Spadina Expressway. At the top of the street are the well-designed Baldwin Steps leading up the escarpment to Casa Loma and Spadina House. On the west sidewalk, from the railway underpass north to the Baldwin Steps, is a work of art by Brad Golden and Norman Richard titled *Spadina Line, 1991*, consisting of bronze words inlaid in the sidewalk and light standards. A plaque explaining the work is on the underpass wall.

The viewing gallery enables visitors to take in the "miles of files" stored at the Archives.

CITY OF TORONTO COLLECTION AND CONSERVATION CENTRE

98 Atlantic Avenue

This old industrial neigh-bourhood is undergoing a significant revival as space is being converted into loft offices, residences, art studios, and homes for new media enterprises.** This four-storey structure was built for the Bank of Commerce in the second decade of the twentieth century as its record and storage centre.

Signs of its once prestigious owner include the bas-relief crest high up on the building front, showing a medallion with ship in full sail-ing gear and three stooks of wheat, the stone bordering the entrance way and windows to either side, and the arched pediment at the roofline. Inside are two of the oldest operable freight elevators in the city.

The former City of Toronto purchased the building several decades ago as a storage, restoration, and conservation facility for art and arti-facts in the City's collection. As is apparent, space is cramped, and the building is open to visitors only on special occasions. Display areas are on the main floor. Since the City amalgamation, a shortage of funds has severely strained the management and protection of heritage concerns. Thus, the Marine Museum—the third most popular of the City's muse-ums in terms of attendance—was closed in 2000 and its artifacts and displays moved here for storage.

Just down the street, at 60 Atlantic Avenue, is Artscape, an innova-tive program of the former City of Toronto to create live-in art studios at affordable rents. On the roof is a sculpture like an air-raid siren titled *Can You Hear What I See?* by Mitchell Fenton. A second Fenton piece is on an Artscape building at 900 Queen Street West, titled *Can You Hear It Too?*

FORT YORK

100 Garrison Road

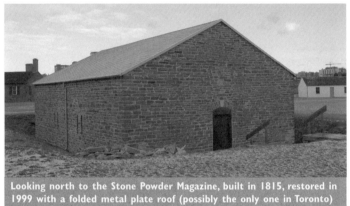

Looking north to the Stone Powder Magazine, built in 1815, restored in 1999 with a folded metal plate roof (possibly the only one in Toronto) and a reproduction of the George III keystone.

John Graves Simcoe, lieutenant-governor of Upper Canada, decided in 1793 to establish a centre of government at some remove from the American border. He chose a site on a harbour protected by the long spit of land, part of the parcel acquired for £1700 by the British in 1787 through the "Toronto purchase," and named it York, in honour of the Duke of York, a son of George III.

A small fort, triangular in shape, was established at the western entrance to the harbour, fitting neatly between the lake and a bend of a stream—appropriately named Garrison Creek—as it entered the bay. Its guardianship of the harbour entrance was complemented by structures on Gibraltar Point on the other side of the gap. The Town of York had grown to some two hundred souls by the time Simcoe returned to England in 1796.

The British spent little on this fortification in the early years. When the Americans invaded in 1813, they burned the fort to the ground before heading east to put the torch to a number of structures in the town, including the Parliament buildings. (In retaliation, British troops burned down the president's house, which was later rebuilt, whitewashed, and called the White House.) After this incident, in the knowledge that Napoleon dominated Europe and that the American navy in Lake Ontario was strong, the British gave more serious thought to defence and created a larger fort. Two gunpowder magazines were built, one in brick and one in stone, as well as brick barracks for officers and soldiers and large wooden blockhouses, which were sufficient to discourage further attacks by the Americans. Seven of these structures still remain, and they are among the oldest buildings in Toronto.

It is dismaying to realize how badly this site has been treated by city leaders in the intervening two centuries. Early in the twentieth century, the city attempted to ram a streetcar line through the site but, led by the artist C. W. Jefferys waving a cartoon with a shadowy streetcar and

Interior of the North Brick Soldiers' Barracks showing one of two restored barracks rooms. This is the 1812 barracks. The other is restored to the 1837 Rebellion period.

the words "The spirit of 1812—Halt!," citizens pushed that threat off the rails. In the 1950s as City Council dreamed of a waterfront covered with expressways, the Gardiner Expressway was planned to pass through the Fort. This threat too was fended off, but thirty years later, Metro Toronto again tried to build a massive interchange joining the Gardiner to Front Street directly over the Fort. That one was arrested as well.

The change in the area surrounding the fort has been considerable, and too often it seems the city has tried to forget this important remnant of its past. Bathurst Street to the east, the Gardiner, and a great deal of landfill to the south have obscured the fact that the south edge of the Fort once rested on the shoreline of Lake Ontario. To the north, the railway tracks have hidden Garrison Creek, which once flowed here. Plans were prepared in the mid-1990s to restore some of the waterway that had once been accessible by boat as far north as Bloor Street. The creek's ravine reached depths of sixty-five feet and in places was twice as wide, but it has been filled with city garbage and soil removed to build the Bloor–Danforth subway line in the 1960s. Remnants of the creek still exist as parks (Trinity Bellwoods Park in the south, Christie Pits in the north) and the bridges crossing it at Harbord and Crawford Streets are in place, although their bulk lies buried. Sadly, the plans remain unrealized as the newly amalgamated city has turned to other priorities.

And the threats continue with development proposed on the south edge of the Fort that will crowd in from that direction. A group called the Friends of Fort York has worked hard to ensure that land use around it is appropriate, but trying to protect the past from the present and the future is no easy task. Happily, the managers of Fort York regularly present a series of events with military themes and showing social life from the early nineteenth century. Fort York needs the prominence—and the appropriate federal support—given to a place like Fort Henry in Kingston. It is one of the city's most important historical artifacts.

The Historic Kitchen in the Officers Brick Barracks and Mess Establishment. This kitchen was part of an 1826 addition to the original 1815 building.

401 RICHMOND

401 Richmond Street West

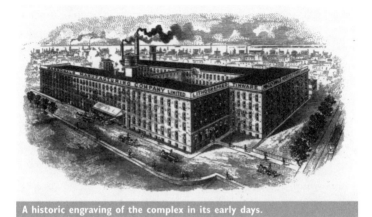

A historic engraving of the complex in its early days.

L ike many other buildings around Spadina, between Queen and King, 401 Richmond was constructed for industrial purposes. A firm of tinwear lithographers occupied the first portion, built in 1889, and as its business expanded it added another four stages, resulting in the existing structure. As the years rolled on, the business changed, and unrelated uses crept in until the building became occupied by an assortment of enterprises looking for inexpensive rental space.

During the 1960s and early 1970s the garment industry was located around this section of Spadina Avenue, providing jobs for new immigrants to Toronto. But that industry too began to move out of the downtown, even out of Ontario altogether. New industries found that the old structures did not serve their needs, and as existing businesses expanded or purchased new equipment, they often found it was easier to move to suburban locations. In the 1970s City Council tried to encourage industries to stay here and implemented a zoning policy permitting only industrial uses in the area. But that led to many unforeseen questions: were companies that processed film considered to be industries, even though the zoning bylaw did not specifically refer to film activity? Were firms creating software for computers industries? Were artists who used space as studios industrialists?

The debates were not resolved to anyone's satisfaction, and a vast amount of unused space opened up in old industrial buildings. Many suggested demolition as a strategy, although the zoning restrictions prevented anything new except unwanted factory structures. But the demand for space changed the situation. As computers grew in popularity in the early 1980s, many kinds of companies offering electronic services found this neighbourhood really interesting. One building on Spadina attracted about a dozen art galleries. By the early 1990s it was clear that new uses for large industrial spaces was a real possibility.

In 1994 Margie Zeidler, architect and daughter of the architect Eb Zeidler, purchased 401 Richmond and drew on all the emerging enterprises to fill the building with a variety of tenants—over 130 of them—particularly artists and other cultural enterprises and computer-related activities. The different users thrive on one others' energy and innovation,

The courtyard.

401 Richmond as it is today.

providing the kind of interaction Jane Jacobs, author and urbanist, thinks is so critical for urban economic health and for the creative process. Zeidler has added a day-care centre (using a small courtyard as the playground), a glass elevator, and a rooftop garden that produces much of the fresh produce used in the Loftus Lloyd café on the main floor. Care has been taken with internal views along the corridors.

As 401 Richmond was establishing itself in the middle of the 1990s, the city decided to rethink the land-use controls that had been in the area for twenty years. Clearly, the industrial designation had protected many structures; however, zoning did not encourage the kinds of activity found in places like 401 Richmond, or new housing, the demand for which seemed insatiable in the downtown. Then-mayor Barbara Hall pulled together a small committee that included Jane Jacobs and the architect and urban designer Ken Greenberg, and the committee proposed that the City should take a very unusual step: abandon all controls over uses of properties, leaving those decisions to the owner, and control only height and setback from the sidewalk. These changes meant that this neighbourhood could be like a European city, where such diverse uses as a medical clinic, a small hotel, an office, a residence could all be within the confines of a single building like 401 Richmond, or on the same block.

The radical new planning regulations have been in place since 1997 and have been extraordinarily effective. New buildings are being built to fit in with existing ones, and owners are attempting to mimic the successful mix of users that has occurred at 401 Richmond.

GEORGE BROWN HOUSE

186 Beverley Street (at Baldwin)

The entrance hall.

This fine, large three-storey structure captures the optimism of the Victorian era and its sense that the world was overflowing with energy and good things. It was built in 1874 for George Brown, who had made a financial success of *The Globe*, the newspaper he founded three decades earlier.

Brown was a voice for Reform politics, first running for public office against William Lyon Mackenzie in 1851, although Mackenzie, who had just returned from exile, was the victor. Brown was elected in a subsequent by-election that year, and he became an inventive advocate of the dissolution of Upper and Lower Canada. The Durham Report of 1841 had forcibly joined together Upper Canada (Ontario) and Lower Canada (Quebec), but Brown and others felt Ontario's interests were given short shrift. He proposed instead a federated structure with significant powers for Ontario and Quebec and relatively limited ones at the national level, although as federation discussions ensued, his position softened. In the famous painting of the Fathers of Confederation—a copy of which may be seen in the basement of the house—he sits in a chair this side of the table, his legs jauntily crossed, looking out of the scene. He saw himself as an opponent of John A. Macdonald, and he wouldn't have been happy with today's strong national government.

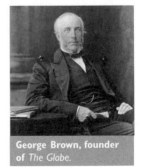

George Brown, founder of *The Globe*.

The first floor of George Brown House—Brown originally called it Lambton Lodge—is both impressive and elegant, with walnut canopies over the doors (note the carved lions from the Brown family coat of arms), a broad sweeping staircase, many fireplaces, and the same floor of patterned tile seen in University College and the central section of Osgoode Hall, both built in the same period. The dining room is in the Art Nouveau style (with a William Morris wallpaper), remodelled by the family that purchased the house from the Browns in 1889.

George Brown died in this building. He was shot at work by a disgruntled—perhaps deranged—employee of The Globe who had been dismissed. The wound was not serious enough to prevent Brown from walking home the several blocks from the Globe offices, but as was common at the time, septic poisoning set in, and Brown died, in bed, about six weeks later.

The house has two sets of stairs for the two sets of people resident in the house in its early years—the generous ones inside the front door for the Brown family, and the narrow ones at the back of the building for the servants, leading to their modest rooms. There are various rooms in the large basement, and a maze of pipes that originally provided heat and gas for the lighting. Gaslights still function in Brown's study, to the right of the main door. Overlooking the third floor at the back is a stained-glass window in greens, blues, red, and gold.

The building was used as a soldiers' rehabilitation centre by the Canadian Institute for the Blind following the First World War until the mid-1950s, when it became the home of the National Association for Retarded Children until the mid-1980s. It then sat vacant for a few years until rescued by the Ontario Heritage Foundation and rehabilitated. Today the basement and main floor are used for meetings, conferences, and social gatherings, and the top two floors are rented out as office space. Editorial offices for two of Canada's most influential literary magazines, *Brick* and *Descant*, are found here, as are offices for the United Empire Loyalists and the Ontario Museum Association. It is a good example of how a building of historical and architectural importance can be fixed up and made available for semi-public use in a cost-efficient manner.

GRADUATE HOUSE

60 Harbord Street

To *Toronto Life* magazine, Graduate House is "a swashbuckling piece of urbanism that wouldn't look out of place in Berlin."

Since it opened in 2000, there has probably been no building in Toronto that has caused such continuous comment as Graduate House, the new residence for four hundred University of Toronto graduate students.

Perhaps controversy was caused because the site is in the midst of an attractive nineteenth-century neighbourhood and the building is completely unrelated in style, or perhaps it's because the building so effectively embodies the provocative architecture being experimented with in a much less successful manner in other parts of the city.

The Spadina side of the architect Stephen Teeple's building consists of two walls rising about ten storeys, each at a different angle to the street. Between them is a stairway that leads, one discovers, not to a courtyard providing light and air into the interior of the building but to a sunken area over which the building seems to close in. This lower yard is surrounded by a water feature, functioning like a moat. On the west side a wooden bench juts out over the water, as though it is an oversight—that portion certainly can't be used for sitting; indeed, even the accessible part of the bench is not comfortable. In the north moat is a cutout moose sculpture by Charles Pachter. Rising above this confined space is the roofline of the north segment. It is highly irregular in shape, hinting vaguely at the tradition of a peak, sheathed in what seem to be leftover sheets of tin patched together. This shaky, uncertain form and cladding is given even more play on the outside north wall of the building.

The Harbord Street facade is much different. Half of the surface is clad in metal on a superstructure that is not quite attached to the building. (The same metal cladding covers the east side of the building, up the laneway.) The exposed part of the building on Harbord at Spadina is painted a dirty grey, and windows peek out through horizontal strips of concrete. At the top a kind of gallery extending over Harbord contains a sign identifying the University of Toronto. The letters are etched on glass, except for the final big metal *O*, which appears to be precariously perched over the middle of the street. These elements of post-modernist architecture challenge accepted Modernist ideas about what successful buildings might look like, and they do so in interesting and provocative ways.

The interior is traditional, providing living space along a double-loaded corridor (rooms on both sides). The ground-floor bistro—sPaHa, obviously named after the two intersecting streets—has been recognized by the avant-garde magazine *Wallpaper** for its minimalist design in tones of grey and silver and the walls of glass, behind which diners can observe, as W. B. Yeats put it, what is past, and passing, and is to come.

Any doubts about the quality of the architecture of Graduate House are quickly dispelled if one looks on the south side of Harbord, at Fort Jock, as the University of Toronto Athletic Building is affectionately known. This structure embodies pure form and extra-large structural elements, everything some Modernist dreamed of, at a scale out of touch with human beings. One's returning gaze then welcomes the challenges of Graduate House, with its lingering sense of incompleteness.

THE GRANGE

Grange Park (John Street, north of Queen)

D'Arcy Boulton Jr., a leading member of the Family Compact, purchased land in 1808 to build a house for his new bride, herself from one of Upper Canada's leading families. But war broke out in 1812 and it was not until 1817 that construction could begin on what we now know as the Grange, the oldest brick building in the city. It is in a straightforward Georgian design, although made of red brick rather than stone, and bears many similarities to Justice William Campbell's house.

Here, the upper windows are two-thirds of the height of those on the ground floor; the pediment window is round rather than elliptical (the transom window is semicircular); and the porch is larger, with a veritable forest of fluted stone columns. Viewed from the south, the building seems to sit on a small rise of land with two sets of steps before those leading to the porch. The house gives the Grange Park an aura of solemnity and quiet, perhaps because the park was the Grange's private estate.

Boulton and his family resided in the house until his death in 1846. It passed to his widow, then to his son William Henry, then to his son's widow, Harriette, who ultimately married Dr. Goldwin Smith, in 1875. Smith, who had made a reputation before leaving England for Canada, was the city's leading intellectual, known as "the Sage of the Grange." One change he made to the front of the building was the replacement of the wooden porch with the essentially identical stone porch that is still evident. He also added a library on the west of the house, slightly recessed from the front wall.

Sir Edmund Walker, a farm boy who became president of the Bank of Commerce and was involved with the National Gallery of Canada and the Royal Ontario Museum, wished to establish an Art Museum of Toronto. He had prevailed on the Smiths to will The Grange to the museum for this purpose. After Smith died in 1910, a committee that

The Grange today, built into the Art Gallery of Ontario (the glass wall of the gallery is visible behind the house, on either side of the pediment).

included the painter George Reid founded the Art Museum of Toronto. Its first exhibit on the premises was held in what is now called the Music Room, upstairs, in 1913. Plans to build proceeded, and the architect Frank Darling was retained. The gallery he designed just north of the Grange opened in 1920, and its first exhibit was the work of the then-controversial Group of Seven.

The new art gallery threw the Grange into a shadow, where it languished for almost fifty years. In the early 1970s, Mary Alice Stuart, a volunteer at the Art Galley of Ontario (as the institution is now called), created the impetus and collected funds to restore the building as a gentleman's house of the mid-nineteenth century. She later became Chair of the Grange Restoration Committee. The restoration by the architect Peter Stokes resulted in some internal changes, including rebuilding the open curved Georgian staircase that Goldwin Smith had replaced with an enclosed one. The interior, which was carefully refurbished with 1830s decor and furniture by Jeanne Minhinnick, consultant on historic houses, has a real elegance. Immediately inside the front door is a large portrait of William Henry Boulton, by the

This photo of Goldwin Smith was taken in his library in December 1909. He would die in this room only six months later (CTA 1244-2150).

nineteenth-century Canadian artist G. T. Berthon. To the left is the dining room, fully set for a meal, and to the right a drawing (as in "with-drawing" after a meal) room. The drawing room and the room behind were probably subdivided in Boulton's day to provide space for children. The hallway is framed by columns, two of which are free-standing, and a considerable portion of the floor space beyond was probably added after the house was originally built. The hallway to the left leads to Smith's library suite, which had its own entrance way so he could hold court without disturbing his wife. The library itself is a fine, high room, with light from the windows on the south wall and bookcases on the north. Smith's portrait, by the Canadian artist J. W. L. Forster, is over the fireplace.

> Greg Gatenby recounts in Toronto: A Literary Guide that Goldwin Smith hosted the poet Matthew Arnold in the Grange, and that Benjamin Disraeli, the British prime minister, detested Smith so much that he made him a pompous character in his novel Lothair. Recognizing himself, Smith complained to Disraeli of the portrait but received no response.

The kitchen was in the basement, and it continues to function as it did in the first half of the nineteenth century. Up the main curved staircase, one passes a portrait of Boulton's father to enter a large central hallway that gives access to a number of rooms. As on the main floor, many of the smaller rooms have been incorporated into larger rooms for entertaining—unlike the Boultons, the Smiths had no children.

During Doors Open, the building can be entered from the porch, but at other times the main access is through the Art Gallery, since the two structures are joined together, and the Grange is often used for exhibits.

The six acres to the south of the Grange is now a public park. On the east side is a red-brick bath house familiar to the architectural style of Toronto of the 1920s, and one of the few still standing in the city. At the south end of the park is the bell tower of the church of St. George the Martyr, all that remains of the original church building destroyed by fire in 1955.

Beyond the southeast corner of the park is University Settlement House, established to reflect the English and American movement of engaging well-educated youth from the universities in the "uplift-ing" of the poor, an impetus that led to the social gospel movement in Canada.

HART HOUSE

7 Hart House Circle

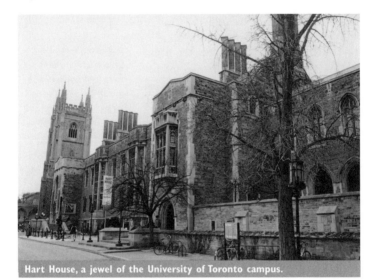

Hart House, a jewel of the University of Toronto campus.

The Massey family has left many architectural legacies in Toronto, mostly resulting from funds available from the estate of Hart Massey (he died in 1896) and the foundation established several decades later with the wealth his companies generated manufacturing farm machinery. Hart Massey's children, including Chester and Lillian, played important roles in these construction enterprises, but perhaps the greatest honour goes to Chester's son Vincent Massey, later Canada's first native-born governor general, a position that he used to substantially enhance culture and the arts in Canada.

Vincent attended the University of Toronto and then Oxford University in England, where he grew to love British traditions, which he brought back to Canada. With the family's support and funding from Hart's estate reorganized as the Massey Foundation, his first sponsorship was Burwash Hall, at Victoria College. Begun in 1909, it is a neo-Gothic structure that serves as the dining hall for the student residence. The next venture was Hart House, which combines in one structure the functions of a cultural, social, and athletic facility. The architectural firm Sproatt & Rolph, designers of Burwash Hall, was retained for Hart House before the Great War and construction began in 1911, but the building's completion was delayed until 1919.

There is a certain English quality to the structure, perhaps revealed in the subdued Gothic influences, the rough grey sandstone (dressed limestone is used at the corners and around the windows), the green slate on the roof, and the tall chimneys. The facade has an easy rhythm about it, stretching from the Soldier's Tower east to the massive form of the Great Hall and its stubby turrets.

The main door opens into a dark cloister-like foyer with stone stairways on all sides. Climbing a few steps, one sees on the right the long hallway of Italian travertine and to the left a common room. Immediately ahead, the windows opening on the central quadrangle light the main rotunda. The spacious hallways provide a clear order to the building, making it exceptionally easy to navigate. Walking to the east toward the Great Hall, one passes by two commodious common rooms with comfortable chairs and couches. On the left are several offices and a small chapel.

The hallway leads to the entrance of the Great Hall, one of the grand spaces in Toronto. The lower portion of the walls—in fact, the first thirteen feet—is covered with Austrian oak panelling, above which, around the whole perimeter of the room, is a quote from John Milton's

The Great Hall.

The art in Hart House is plentiful and varied and has been purchased since 1922 by the Art Committee, one of the many committees of students and faculty established by Hart House to participate in the management of the facility. The first painting purchased was by A. Y. Jackson, *Georgian Bay, November*. The collection includes paintings by Tom Thomson, Emily Carr, Charles Comfort, David Milne, and Carl Schaefer. Many contemporary pieces grace the walls and hallways, as the collection continues to expand.

The Debates Room.

"Areopagitica," his essay against censorship, written in 1644. On the north and south walls are university crests. A large fireplace occupies much of the north wall. Gothic-style windows on the upper portion of the room open on the west side to an upper gallery rather than to the outside world. The shallow arched wooden ceiling is supported by intricately carved beams of American oak. Stone corbels are found just below the ceiling, often using the letter *H* and incorporating caricatures of Vincent Massey, his wife, Alice, and of the architects. This hall is used on a daily basis for meals and has fortunately become a familiar part of the experience of many university students. Just outside the Great Hall one has a fine view of the quadrangle and the many sculptures that dot it.

Upstairs, the Debates Room is large, with a more formal and less intimidating wooden ceiling. Photographs on the wall show some of the many debates held here over the years when debating was an important way of airing issues of the day, before the debasement of such discussion through television. Women are notably absent from the images; Hart House policy until the 1970s excluded women, aside from the occasional social event. Happily, this policy was amended and today both sexes use the building.

Farther along the hallway is a comfortable library filled with red-leather couches. The room is often used for students looking for a quiet spot to snooze away a few hours. Also on the second floor is the Music Room, once more with a distinct character of its own. All common rooms in Hart House are filled with Canadian art.

The north wing includes a small art gallery on the ground floor, and facilities focusing on fitness, now that athletics have been relocated to the Athletics Building at Harbord and Spadina.

The Soldier's Tower, added in 1924 as a memorial to the First World War (and later the Second World War) combatants, creates a physical link between the different styles of Hart House and University College. A room located over the archway contains memorabilia from the wars, as well as a stained-glass memorial window.

The south facade of Hart House and the east facade of University College are two sides to a square in which stands the old Observatory, built in 1854. One now marvels that an observatory of such low height functioned so well in a city where ambient light now makes it difficult to see any stars with the naked eye, even on a fairly clear night.

The Library, circa 1930.

LIBERTY GRAND

25 British Columbia Road (Exhibition Place)

Some entrepreneurs are able to make an economically sustainable activity from what others consider a loser—and to do it in a way that looks really easy. Nick Di Donato of the Liberty Entertainment Group did that with his transformation of the Courthouse Market Grille (in the long-vacant York County Court House on Adelaide Street East) and the Rosewater Supper Club (in the former Consumers Gas head office) on Toronto Street. He's at it again here.

The Ontario Government Building at the Canadian National Exhibition was designed by the Toronto architects Chapman & Oxley. With a triangular footprint and an interior courtyard, it is an open, airy building constructed in 1926 in the Beaux-Arts style of reinforced concrete without heating facilities, as it was intended only as a display structure for the government dur-

ing the summer weeks of the Ex. Nevertheless, its style was very grand—a dome crowns the main entrance facing the lake and pairs of cupolas emphasize the corners of the structure. Two columns, in the capitals of which are sculpted bears, and a series of seven tall arched windows flank the central doorway on the south face. The frieze along the top of the building has alternating images of a fisherman's dory surrounded by plump fish, and a stag besieged by hungry hunting dogs. Encrusted on the facade between the windows are scowling lynx heads. Around the corners of the building there are friezes—one showing farmers sowing and reaping; another showing men hunting, a dead stag hanging between them. It's a bit unclear how these emblems of the Canadian wilderness fitted with the sculptures of Greek figures (they are in concrete and several figures are repeated from the same mould) but the exuberance of the scene dispels qualms about coherence. Two recumbent lions protect the entrance on the lake side. On the northeast corner is the dedication by Howard Ferguson, then premier of Ontario, and members of his cabinet.

But this interesting exterior was not equalled inside, where services and finishes were minimal—all the attention had been given to outside presentation in the knowledge that displays would fill the interior. Because the nature of the Ex has changed

Two plaques grace the plinths where lions sit on the building's south side. One marks the death of Captain McNeal, Donald Maclean, other soldiers, "and Indians" in a battle against the Americans in the War of 1812, "in defence of the capital of Upper Canada." The other is a bas-relief of a young woman swimming, dedicated to the sixteen-year-old Marilyn Bell for her "magnificent athletic feat of swimming the full width of Lake Ontario," September 9, 1954.

The Ontario Government Building (now the Liberty Grand), circa 1930 (CTA 1244-2024).

and the province no longer mounts exhibits, in the past few decades the neglected building became tawdry and unpleasant. The Liberty Entertainment Group has gone to considerable trouble to re-create a stylish venue.

The space has been converted into large elegant ballrooms appropriate for banquets, celebrations, and presentations. Detail has been added to the inside of the arches on the south face to match the splendid exterior. Columns have been constructed to provide continuity to the rooms, and in some cases the moose and lynx heads in the capitals have been duplicated. The ceilings of British Columbia fir—twenty-seven feet above the floor—have been tastefully decorated, and tulip-shaped chandeliers modelled after those placed in the Pavilion at Versailles in the 1920s seem entirely at home. Rugs and colour schemes make the rooms warm and inviting.

What is intriguing about the changes made in the past year, after the building had suffered so much neglect, is how right the renovations seem as a way to showcase the qualities of the structure that Chapman & Oxley had designed, and how appropriate the new use is for this space.

The Governor's Room, the largest of three ballrooms within the complex.

PRINCESS OF WALES THEATRE

300 King Street West

The success of the Royal Alexandra Theatre and the opportunities the impresarios Ed and David Mirvish found to fill other large performance spaces in Toronto led them to create a new theatre, the first privately developed large venue in the city in many decades. The renowned Toronto theatre architect Peter Smith was retained, and he designed this magnificent one on a very small site. It was named after Diana, Princess of Wales, and opened in May 1993.

The building sits rather modestly at the edge of King Street, its facade a relatively simple mixture of metal, glass, and stone, all in elegant, soft colours. Brushed-steel columns on the upper floor are a nice design surprise. From the outside one can hardly imagine how spectacular the building is inside.

The interior public areas are designed by Yabu Pushelberg, a renowned Toronto firm of interior designers. The profusion of artwork constantly catches the eye: tile mosaics, blown-glass lamps, unique metal light fixtures and warm mahogany dressing the doors, archways, and the bar. Based on examples from the seventeenth century, the hall is ringed with seats; the line of the balconies is continued through to the proscenium by boxes. This design embodies the notion that theatre is best when the stage is completely surrounded by the audience, without a break, enhancing the connection between performers and viewers. The mural on the proscenium arch and the ceiling dome is by the American artist Frank Stella. Before joining his father, Ed, in theatrical endeavours, David Mirvish ran an important art gallery on Markham Street. His friendship with Stella comes from that period. On the exterior wall at the rear of the theatre on Pearl Street is another large work by Stella, similar to those found inside.

The construction of the building did not go entirely smoothly. The Mirvishes wished to open as quickly as possible to accommodate the Broadway hit *Miss Saigon*. Another theatre producer in Toronto at the time, Garth Drabinsky, who used a municipally owned theatre in North York for his productions, was determined to stand in their way. He objected to the waiver of parking requirements that the Mirvishes had obtained from the city, and to avoid the delay Drabinsky's objection would cause, the Mirvishes decided to build the required parking and swallow the several millions in cost needed to proceed. Drabinsky's career as a theatre mogul has since come to an unceremonious end.

To the east is a modest structure covered in white tile, the Anderson Building. One of the delights of Toronto is simply stopping and looking to see what is there—and coming across something as fine as the Anderson Building, fitting comfortably with its next-door neighbour, the Princess of Wales Theatre.

The interior of the theatre was designed by the award-winning firm of Yabu Pushelberg.

ROY THOMSON HALL

🏛 60 Simcoe Street

In the 1970s serious music lovers in Toronto looked long and hard for an alternative to Massey Hall that could become a more comfortable home of the Toronto Symphony Orchestra and the Toronto Mendelssohn Choir. A site at King and Simcoe was purchased from Canadian Pacific Railway as part of the Metro Centre development (which later failed).

This had once been a very important corner in the city. Here stood the province's lieutenant-governor's residence and across the street to the north was the original Upper Canada College. Across the street to the east stood (and still stands) St. Andrew's Church, and kittycorner, a tavern—the intersection of Legislation, Education, Salvation, and Damnation, as it was described.

The Vancouver architect Arthur Erickson was retained to provide an innovative design for the concert hall. He offered an oval building covered in glass, with curvilinear walls, which make the building a delight to look at in the evening as the interior light radiates through the glass. Some have quarrelled about the appropriateness of this form for a musical facility. Over the centuries architects have developed very precise formulae for the creation of space that seats several thousand people to allow them to hear the music played. This building, which opened in 1982, seems not to have incorporated many of these formulae. Acoustic problems have bedevilled it, and plans are now under way to spend some $20 million on improvements.

The marquee over the door on Simcoe Street is small, and the upper door jamb running the length of Simcoe Street is under seven feet from the ground, so that walking through often makes a visitor reflexively stoop—these may be the lowest main doors of any building in the city. The lobby is very inviting, swathed in elegant greys, and the stainless steel of the railings, doors, and fixtures gleam, and mirrors reflect the activity of the crowd. This is an excellent place to see and be seen. The auditorium is dressed in the same elegant grey, and while all 2,812 seats are commodious, everyone is within about a hundred feet from the stage.

A sunken reflection pool separates the Hall from King Street, and unfortunately creates a large chunk of dead space, which demeans

the experiences of the considerable number of pedestrians attracted to the Hall and the two premier performing venues on the north side of King. Good design should enhance a sense of urban excitement and engagement.

Roy Thomson Hall is named after the Canadian publisher who, before the era of Rupert Murdoch, owned more newspapers in the world than anyone else. Following what has quickly become the key fundraising mechanism for performance spaces, both artistic and athletic, his family contributed the first 10 per cent of the cost of the building on condition that his name be attached to it.

Inside the auditorium.

ROYAL ALEXANDRA THEATRE

260 King Street West

Opened in 1907, the "Royal Alex" is one of the oldest continuously operating theatres in North America.

In the early 1900s, Cawthra Mulock, a successful Toronto businessman, assembled some of his friends to invest in a new theatre for touring productions from New York and London. A New York firm was first approached for drawings, and when it was clear that a Toronto architect would be needed, the job was given to John M. Lyle, who had grown up in Hamilton but was then working in New York. Lyle returned to Toronto to begin a prosperous and influential career, championing the City Beautiful Movement. His first work was the Royal Alexandra Theatre, in 1906.

Lyle's design has three parts: at the rear, the tall brick stage block to house backstage devices; in the middle, the relatively plain exterior of the theatre box; and on the street, the elegant grey stone entrance in Beaux-Arts style. Note the stone medallion gracing the parapet at the top of the building, just in front of the recessed mansard roof. The marquee is large and when lit adds a real sense of excitement to the entrance.

The main doors lead comfortably (although perhaps by today's standards snugly) to the glorious theatre itself, which has been admiringly

The City Beautiful Movement, in which John Lyle played a prominent part, had as its objective improving the downtown with wide, graceful avenues (on the order of Baron Haussmann's Second Empire Paris), and handsome public buildings, perhaps like the Royal Alex. Plans were drawn up for several new streets, but University Avenue is the only realized example, and even there the plan was not fully implemented: a round-about and surrounding buildings were not built.

referred to as a jewel box. The proscenium is covered in decorated plaster and the stage hidden by a royal red curtain and a gold-embossed surcover. Above the proscenium arch is a mural by Frederick S. Challener titled *Aphrodite Discovering Adonis*, a fine reversal of the more usual man-spying-on-woman story. To the sides are regal boxes. The curve of the rows of seats at all three levels is generous (although the leg room is not), and all audience members are made to feel close to the stage. To accomplish this, the second balcony has been built at a very steep pitch. The lighting in the theatre makes the whole space sparkle with anticipation and opulence, fitting for a building named after an English princess.

Mulock's investment quickly paid off, and the theatre was a success for more than fifty years. Then with the coming of television and the opening of the more sophisticated and modern O'Keefe Centre in 1960, the Royal Alex (as it is commonly known) languished. Many feared the building would be demolished when it was put up for sale in 1963, but it was unexpectedly purchased by Ed Mirvish. Mirvish had made his fortune running his innovative cut-rate department-store emporium, Honest Ed's, at Bloor and Bathurst, and theatre acquisition looked like a strange detour for him. But Mirvish renovated the building and instituted a subscription system that filled it with Torontonians who thought they had lost the practice of regular theatre-going, making this one of the oldest continually operating theatres in the country. Many of the plays were performed by touring companies from New York or Britain, just as Mulock had planned, but Mirvish's investment revitalized Toronto theatre and the public cultural life of the city. Today most productions feature local talent.

Mirvish then purchased the surrounding warehouses, which he converted into popular restaurants for ticket-holders. In the ensuing forty years, he relinquished his restaurant enterprises to other entrepreneurs, and he and his son, David, have devoted themselves to theatre. He purchased and rebuilt the Old Vic, an important theatre in London, England, to great acclaim, and in the early 1990s built the Princess of Wales, just to the west of the Royal Alex.

Among the hundreds of performers who have taken to this stage are John Gielgud, Orson Welles, Ruth Gordon, Al Jolson, Humphrey Bogart, Mary Pickford, Fred and Adele Astaire, Edith Piaf, the Marx Brothers, and Mae West.

ROYAL CANADIAN MILITARY INSTITUTE

426 University Avenue

T he Canadian Military Institute was established late in the nineteenth century in a house on Simcoe Street. The building now on University Avenue is an extension of the original, along with additions and alterations made to create the illusion that it was originally constructed to front on University Avenue. Perhaps it is the pair of nine-pound muzzle-loading cannon that give the building a sense of permanence and longevity; perhaps it is the added columns stretching from the foundation to the cornice that make it feel old.

In 1948 Royal was added to the Institute's name, giving royal blessing to the service of many Canadians in the First and Second World Wars. The Institute was the venue for them to gather, mourn their friends, and celebrate their contribution to the country. The RCMI has the largest privately funded military library on the continent, with forty thousand volumes covering ancient to recent history. It is open by appointment to serious scholars. The Ward Room honours the navy and appears like part of a ship; the Wing Room commemorates the air force. Throughout the building there are displays of crests, medals, swords, paintings, and other artifacts. The complex serves as a club for those with military interest and experience, providing several lounges, dining rooms, a billiard room, and a number of bedrooms for overnight guests.

This small, strong, but modest structure seems as much out of place on University Avenue as does the University Club just to the south. From the days of the City Beautiful Movement, city planners have dreamed of making University Avenue into one of the city's premier processional streets, lined by important and distinguished buildings. Special bylaws were put in place to ensure a dignified form and cladding for new buildings and to prevent retail and restaurant uses at grade, as they were considered déclassé. These efforts have created a street that seems dull and uninspiring, showing the heavy hand of the planning bureaucracy.

Between the street's rivers of traffic lies a strange garden-like boulevard laid out with good intentions, but it is not a particularly pleasant place to walk. Sculptures dot it, including one just north of the Institute dedicated to British airmen of the Second World War and mockingly referred to as "Gumby Goes to Heaven." A fine monument to Adam Beck, the founder of the publicly owned electrical system in Ontario, is several blocks north, at College Street.

One of the two British nine-pound smoothbore, muzzle-loading cannon that stand in front of the building.

ROYAL CONSERVATORY OF MUSIC

273 Bloor Street West

This structure was originally the Toronto Baptist College, built in 1880. Henry Langley's architecture firm was used, as he had forged a special relationship with the Baptists, including designing the Jarvis Street Baptist Church (at Gerrard Street) in 1874, and a house for the successful merchant William McMaster, who provided the funds for this building.

The Baptist College moved to Hamilton in 1930 to join McMaster University; the building then came under the control of the University of Toronto. In 1968 the Conservatory of Music building at the southwest corner of University and College was demolished (to be replaced by the Ontario Hydro building), and the Conservatory moved here.

The building is only five storeys high, but the design elements make it feel higher: the front door is a dozen steps above grade, all the lines in the building are vertical, the steeply pitched roof is studded with dormers, and above are tall chimneys. The surface is an odd mixture of dark red stone and red brick, with the latter used to create the vertical elements. Unfortunately, the brick is in need of repair.

A brick porch with a large arch supported by polished marble columns stands at the main entrance. The porch is almost two storeys high, providing much focus on this door. To the east, the building bulges out toward Bloor Street, a familiar Victorian device to indicate that the world is filled to overflowing with God's goodness. Beyond that, the walls of a simple Romanesque chapel, only half the height of the main structure, protrude to the sidewalk. The windows of the chapel on its west and Bloor Street sides have been bricked over, but its simple elegance remains.

Immediately inside the front doors, the entrance way is red and yellow brick with black-tarred brick for decoration. In all likelihood the interior hallways, also in brick, had the same warm and decorative quality, but the brick has been painted, giving a ho-hum feel to the interior. The fine arches over interior doors leave no doubt that considerable care was originally taken to create a comfortable and beautiful space.

The Royal Conservatory of Music has illustrious alumni, including Glenn Gould, Teresa Stratas, Liona Boyd, Jon Vickers, and David Foster.

The corridor to the left leads to a pleasant sitting room with a bay window. Exhibited here are paintings of Edward Fisher, founder of the Toronto Conservatory of Music in 1886; Sir Ernest Macmillan, a leading conductor and musician in the city in the mid-twentieth century, done by Cleeve Horne in a 1950s style; and a fine painting of an unidentified pianist by Kenneth Forbes. This room leads to the former chapel, converted in 1997 to the comfortable Ettore Mazzoreni Hall, seating several hundred. The peaked roof is a dominant element in this space. Windows on the east side of the hall are clear glass, surely not what Langley had intended, and the bricking of other windows—undoubtedly to prevent outside noise from leaking in—appears to have been done with considerably more taste than on the exterior.

It is worth retracing one's steps to the central stairways and ascending a level or two to hear the music seeping from rehearsal rooms and offices, and to view the woodwork of the original stairway on the second and third floors—one wishes it had not been abandoned on the lower level. The landings give access to the stair tower of the addition

Glenn Gould, an admired alumnus of the Conservatory, in rehearsal in Toronto, 1974.

to the rear. This tower is a strange construction, cramped and curving five storeys high, even though the addition itself is but three storeys. Another addition is tacked onto the southeast corner of the main building.

East is Philosopher's Walk, leading to Hoskin Avenue. This was the course of Taddle Creek as it made its way from Wychwood Park, near Bathurst and Davenport, down through the current city to this site, then past Eaton's College Street to Moss Park, and into the lake near Parliament and Front Streets. The entrance to Philosopher's Walk is marked by impressive stone gates with decorative ironwork—the Queen Alexandra Gateway, a gift of the Imperial Order of Daughters of the Empire in 1902 to mark a royal visit. It was originally located at the Bloor Street entrance to Queen's Park but was moved here in 1962 to accommodate the widening of University Avenue.

ST. ANNE'S ANGLICAN CHURCH

270 Gladstone Avenue

Father Lawrence Skey, rector of St. Anne's Church in the early years of the twentieth century, was dissatisfied with the traditional Gothic structure in which his congregation worshipped. He dreamed of a building in the Byzantine style, and when the decision was made to demolish the existing structure for something much larger, his wish was granted. A competition was held, and Ford Howland's design was under construction by 1907.

The exterior on Gladstone is plain—three simple doors under a jutting roof, framed by two small towers, entirely dressed in a yellowish brick. The surprise is inside. A wide dome (in fact a dozen feet wider than St. Mark's in Venice) floats on four large arches. The main doors open through the east arch; beyond the west arch is the sanctuary and choir, set in a domed apse broken by five clusters of windows. To the south a large window of stained glass floods the main body of the church with light. More light comes from the lunettes that stud the dome

The nave and sanctuary, decorated in the Byzantine Revival style, evocative of such celebrated churches as St. Mark's in Venice.

In 1923, when finalizing plans for decorating the interior, J. E. H. MacDonald and William Rae, the architect assigned to the scheme, consulted Sir Charles Nicholson, then the architect in charge of St. Paul's Cathedral in London. Nicholson apparently chose the colour scheme that was followed.

St. Mark.

St. Matthew.

above. The church is quite large, originally seating fourteen hundred, now about a thousand. The elements of the structure are similar to the much larger Hagia Sophia in Istanbul, a building that has served as both a Christian and a Muslim place of worship.

The rich decoration is very impressive, and also in the Byzantine style. (Decoration had always been Howland's intention, but funds were not available for this until the early 1920s, when J. E. H. MacDonald of the Group of Seven was retained as chief designer.) The apse over the altar is covered in mosaics (added in 1960) with gold predominating, and panels depicting the life of Christ over the five arches. The triangular paintings between the four arches supporting the building's dome are particularly impressive: *The Crucifixion* by MacDonald to the left of the altar; *The Nativity* by F. H. Varley to the right (in which he apparently depicts himself as a shepherd); *The Ascension* by H. S. Stansfield and the *The Resurrection* by H. S. Palmer on the other pillars. Just above the painted words at the base of the dome are Varley's heads of four Old Testament prophets, and plaques of the Evangelists by Frances Loring and Florence Wyle. The ceiling of the apse is painted in blue, overlaid with vine leaves and clusters of grapes. The detailing and colouring throughout the church is very affecting, a most successful integration of Group of Seven style with Byzantine sensibilities.

SPADINA: HISTORIC HOUSE AND GARDENS

285 Spadina Road

A view of the terrace from the southern lawn.

When Dr. William Warren Baldwin built a small summer home for his family on the top of the escarpment, he named it after the Native term for hill, *espadinong*, Spadina, pronounced "Spadeena." It was a plain two-storey wood frame structure that he had designed himself.

Baldwin was the first medical doctor serving the citizens of York. He married a cousin of Peter Russell, one of the leading members of the Family Compact, the elite that ruled Upper Canada, yet he was generally found on the Reform side of politics. His son Robert was a moderate Reformer who winced at the antics of William Lyon Mackenzie, and he—rather than Mackenzie, who may indeed be more deserving—is usually credited with the idea of responsible government for Upper Canada.

In 1835 the Spadina house burned down, and Dr. Baldwin moved his family into town. The next year he began work on a new house on the old foundations. In a subdivision of his property holdings south of Bloor Street, he laid out a magnificent thoroughfare to Spadina—a street two chains (132 feet) wide, twice the width of a normal street—and carefully planted it with chestnut trees. He named it Spadina Avenue, and it provided a wonderful vista for his house on the hill.

In 1865 the Baldwin home was auctioned and found its way into the hands of James Austin, a very successful businessman who was president of the Dominion Bank and Consumers Gas. The next year he demolished the second Spadina to make way for a structure worthy of a wealthy Victorian gentleman, the third Spadina, which currently stands on the site.

The plain cream-coloured stucco of the exterior hides the lavish detailing inside. In true Victorian style, it was quite stuffed with couches, tables, chairs, statues, lamps, chandeliers, curtains, patterned wallpaper, paintings, fancy rugs, and mirrors, all in good taste and most of it still here. The property was donated to the City of Toronto in the early 1980s by Anna Kathleen Thompson, an Austin descendant, on the understanding that it would remain mostly an example of the Victorian era, yet a close look reveals the additions from the Arts and Crafts, Art Nouveau and Art Deco styles from the late nineteenth

The drawing room.

century and first few decades of the twentieth. There are many rooms of interest—the conservatory, the billiard room, the walk-in refrigerator, the dining room, and the small room for the telephone. The Austin family was one of the first in the city to have a telephone, although it was of little use until others had one as well. In the basement, archaeological work shows the foundations of the first two Spadina Houses, providing a real sense of human continuity on the site. One can also get

Dr. William Warren Baldwin (1775–1844), the first civilian doctor in York, as well as a lawyer and a self-taught architect.

an understanding of what life might have been like for domestic staff working in the kitchen areas of the basement.

The six-acre property on which Spadina House sits boasts a magnificent series of gardens, including a well-cultivated herb and vegetable garden and an orchard with fruit trees. To the south, the patio steps spill down to an expansive lawn running right to the lip of the escarpment. The size of the oak trees here reflects their lives of three hundred and more years.

Between Spadina House and Casa Loma—a relative newcomer to the area, being built only before the First World War—are the Baldwin Steps, a recent piece of good urban design by the City of Toronto. The steps move down the escarpment in a series of short bursts (with frequent landings), ultimately arriving at Davenport Road, the former shore of Lake Iroquois.

STEAM WHISTLE BREWERY
(CPR ROUNDHOUSE)

255 Bremner Boulevard

Inside the Steam Whistle Brewery.

The city is full of reminders of places and technologies whose time has passed. The Steam Whistle Brewery in the CPR Roundhouse combines two such reminders: steam whistles, which are rarely heard in the city today, and the roundhouse, primarily used for servicing locomotives.

This Roundhouse was designed in 1929 by Anglin–Norcross. It was the only one in the country to use steam technology, with a rotating turntable 120 feet long, strong enough to move a locomotive into a repair or storage bay. When first built, it was part of a 200-acre site devoted entirely to trains, stretching from Bathurst to Yonge and south from Front The passenger tracks were clustered near Front Street, where they had access to Union Station, while freight traffic used the slightly elevated highliner track on the south end. Between these two groupings were all the things necessary to keep trains in good working order: water towers, coach-cleaning facilities, and of course the Roundhouse, where engines and cars could be repaired.

In the 1950s all three levels of government invested heavily in roads and airports—the Gardiner Expressway immediately south of the

Canadian Pacific locomotive #2715, used between Toronto, Hamilton and Buffalo, on the turntable of the Roundhouse.

In the early 1970s, the Metro Centre development was proposed for the railway lands, requiring the demolition of Union Station and moving some tracks to the south to allow for a southerly expansion of the business district. The plan ran into citizen opposition and was largely abandoned. Only one portion of the scheme was actually built, the CN Tower, which serves primarily as a communications device and tourist attraction, one of the tallest free-standing structures in the world.

highliner track is an example. As rail traffic declined, the Roundhouse was used for freight car repair, then for diesel engines. Before long railways were allowed to languish in Canada as a matter of policy (although not in Europe). In 1983 the turntable did its last work, and the Roundhouse officially closed three years later.

The interior of the Roundhouse is astounding for its size: locomotives really were mammoth beasts. The Douglas fir posts, so dominant in the building's post-and-beam construction, have been retained by the renovation architect William Hurst, and the multi-paned windows on the outside of the Roundhouse flood the brick walls with light. Happily, arrangements have been completed to have the Toronto Railway Museum occupy several bays adjacent to the brewery. Part of the exibit will include a steam locomotive.

Bremner Boulevard is named after Ray Bremner, the commissioner of Works in the former City of Toronto in the 1960s until the late '80s.

Aerial view of the Roundhouse, 1974. The base of the CN Tower is visible at the right.

TORONTO CARPET FACTORY

67 Mowat Avenue

A historic sketch of the Toronto Carpet Factory, circa 1899.

In the last few years of the nineteenth century, the Toronto Carpet Company was located at Jarvis and the Esplanade, but it was undergoing considerable growth. In 1899 under the leadership of company president Barry Hayes, originally from Stratford, Ontario, the company embarked on a major expansion, and at the turn of the century moved into its new building here on the south side of King Street.

With an expanding population and a quality product, the company continued to grow, adding its own spinning and carding facilities as well as more looms, which were in the massive structure on Mowat Street, constructed a few years later. During the Great War, the company changed its product to manufacture blankets, then khaki cloth. (The cloth initiative was later spun off into the Barrymore Cloth Company, which in the 1920s became a leading manufacturer of men's and women's clothing.) By the end of the war, the company had expanded to a thousand employees located in a dozen buildings on this four-acre block.

The firm continued to innovate in carpet products for the next five decades, until business began to slow. In the late 1970s, as the surviving members of the Hayes family became too old to provide vibrant management, the business was wound down and its assets were sold. Fortunately, the structures remained intact.

The largest, most impressive building is the five-storey one on Mowat Street. Its height is exaggerated by the red-brick pillars—thirty-five in all—marching down the block. Each pillar is on a stone base and ends at a decorated stone capital just below the stone arches under the cornice. The sashed windows—mostly original—are big, and their gentle arches and many panes add much grace to the facade. Inside, the ceilings stretch as high as twenty-two feet, the hardwood floors are newly cleaned, and the restoration has been sensitive—"invisible mending" is the way the owner, Bob Eisenberg, refers to the rehabilitation.

Just to the east of the Carpet Factory is Lamport Stadium, a soccer field named after Allan Lamport, a flamboyant mayor in the 1950s best known for bringing Sunday sports to Toronto. This was the former site of the Mercer Reformatory for Women.

The building on King Street at Fraser was the first on the site. Again, one notices the red brick, the careful brick piers and windows, and a gently peaked roof. The tower on King Street has a nice reticence about it. The 151-foot smokestack, the building for the enormous steam pump, and other structures are found in the interior of the block—the railway tracks remain from the days when most shipping was done by train, hence the need to locate tracks right at the shipping doors—and their different original uses have allowed interesting configurations for current uses, including a restaurant that may be hidden inside the block off the street but has gained a citywide reputation.

The complex has been renovated for a range of companies, many involved in design, media, and the new electronic environment. Eisenberg was on the committee in the mid-1990s that drew up the new zoning for the King–Spadina area, where the emphasis was put on building form. Use and density controls were generally abandoned so new businesses that didn't fit comfortably within any City bylaws were readily accommodated without the need for City permission. (A fuller description of these new controls is found in the discussion of 401 Richmond Street West.) That same kind of approach has been applied to this block and has helped make it a financial and aesthetic success.

UNIVERSITY COLLEGE

15 King's College Circle

University College is one of the great buildings in Canada. Situated on the main U of T campus, it was designed by Frederic W. Cumberland of Cumberland & Storm in 1856, after a visit to the British Isles. Ruskin's influence is readily apparent in the Gothic elements (also seen in the firm's Chapel of St. James-the-Less, built in the same decade), the reliance on the imaginative power of the workmen to provide rich detail, and the organic form. Fire destroyed the college in 1890, but it was rebuilt as it had been designed.

The building should first be viewed from the south, across King's College Circle. The roofline is in constant flux, with a profusion of towers, turrets, chimneys, iron railings, and pointed protrusions. While there is a common roofline on either side of the central tower, there appears to be deliberate asymmetry within. On the right of the facade, three floors seem to be marked by the three levels of windows. On the left there are but two window levels. This is one of the building's delightful false trails—inside, both wings have only two floors.

The main door is recessed between decorated piers and receding levels of round carved stone arches and columns, each level bearing a different design, as though one layer has been peeled to reveal another and another and another. The world, the entrance seems to say, is complicated and variegated, with many mysteries yet to be discovered. Above the door is a carving of the university crest, with a tree, the lamp of learning and a smiling owl. The piers to either side of the doors are capped by patterned pitched roofs. The inspiration for this entrance derived from the Norman Gate Tower of Bury St. Edmunds, built in the twelfth century. William Storm had borrowed a copy of a book with a drawing of the tower, and there are remarkable similarities between its gateway and this entrance.

Inside, common elements recur and act as thematic agents. First, there is an extraordinary number of columns. Some mark doorways and passageways; some are free-standing supports for arches, to be walked around,

The elaborate main entrance.

University College today.

In his book, The Stones of Venice, published in 1853, just a few years before University College was designed, John Ruskin devoted a lengthy chapter to "The Nature of Gothic."

"Pointed arches do not constitute Gothic," he wrote, "nor vaulted roofs, nor flying buttresses, nor grotesque sculptures; but all or some of these things, and many other things with them, when they come together so as to have life.... [T]he characteristic or moral elements of Gothic are the following, placed in the order of their importance:

1. Savageness
2. Changefulness
3. Naturalism
4. Grotesqueness
5. Rigidity
6. Redundance

These characters are here expressed as belonging to the building; as belonging to the builder, they would be expressed thus: 1. Savageness or Rudeness, 2. Love of Change, 3. Love of Nature, 4. Disturbed Imagination, 5. Obstinacy, 6. Generosity. And I repeat, that the withdrawal of any one, or any two, will not at once destroy the Gothic character of a building, but the removal of a majority of them will."

some frame windows or emerge from the brickwork, only half visible. All have elaborate bases and capitals.

The variety of woodwork is impressive. Many ceilings are wooden, some rough with large timbers, some more refined, some with extra layers, many with a feeling of strength and vitality. Wood panelling is abundant, usually patterned. Several staircases in wood are exceptional. Carvings in wood and stone are breathtaking in their detail, execution, number, and variety, reflecting Ruskin's idea of giving free rein to the worker's energy and imagination.

The stained glass is also exceptional. Only lecture rooms appear to have clear glass—the remaining numerous windows have coloured glass. Windows are typically edged in glass of deep colours, with the main body in a subtle shade of yellow or purple or blue glass. The patterns and colours vary immensely, although windows in the same room at the same level usually have similar designs and colours.

Many people think interior brick walls are a relatively recent discovery, but this building shows that isn't the case. Their yellow brick is warm and solid, an excellent contrast to the grey sandstone and the dark wood panelling.

Inside the main door one is in a small entrance foyer with a patterned tile floor and wooden ceiling. Three steps lead through the narrow entrance way into another anteroom, where there are two sets of columns, the capitals of which are richly carved with human heads and what appear to be turkeys. To either side, broad stone staircases lead to an upper floor. Beyond the columns is the central rotunda. On the north wall are a pair of arched windows at eye level and above, five arches, only three of which have windows. The lower half of the high room is panelled, and faces carved at the top of the panelling are a surprise. A round chandelier hangs from the heavily beamed wooden ceiling. Underfoot is an intricately designed tile floor in red, black, tan, and blue. The height of the room, the colours, the detailing, and the materials all make it feel baronial.

Retreating back through the columns, take the staircase on the right, past the bust of Cumberland looking at those who come to admire his handiwork. The stone steps are wide, the brick walls plain. The view of the rotunda from this second level is impressive. A narrow staircase can be found a few steps to the west, for access to the third floor. A large metal sculpture by Robert Murray dangles precipitously through the atrium in the stairwell, a gift in honour of the architect and historian Eric Arthur. This level opens into a small (almost secret)

The library in East Hall in 1884, six years before it was destroyed in a devastating fire.

The cloister (CTA 1244-3144).

room under the eaves, where heavy beams cross the ceiling and sustain the transom windows that pour light into the room. On the north wall is a large circular stained-glass window. One feels as if in the belly of a whale.

Back on the second floor, there are more riches to discover. To the left is West Hall, a lofty space with a wooden ceiling resting on large carved ribs. The arched windows, in groups of two and three, are placed high in the walls, providing a great flood of light from both the north and south. On the west wall is a rose window of azure blue, dedicated to Marsh Jeanneret, once a principal of University College. Below the windows, the wall is panelled in a dark wood, topped by 266 roundels, small carvings outstanding in variety and execution. These apparently were added after the 1890 fire. Surmounting the doors in West Hall are chubby, friendly bears and sheep holding heraldic shields.

East Hall feels much less celebratory. Three windows loom ominously on the east side, the largest in sombre tones of grey with a hint of gold, showing Queen Victoria dressed like Athena. In the smaller window on the left is a scholar, on the right a soldier. This window was a gift from college alumni following the fire.

Here one finds windows at floor levels—from the outside these had suggested there were three stories to this wing. The panelling is low and unadorned. Above, there are large paired windows on both walls.

The wooden ribbed roof (not as high as West Hall) is supported by beams sitting on exuberantly carved stone piers with animal motifs predominating.

On the main floor, the corridor leading west is in yellow brick, with a ribbed wooden ceiling. It leads to a broad wooden stairway under a thick-beamed wooden ceiling and a large carved newel post. At the top of the stairway, a red, blue, and silver stained-glass window gives the space a medieval feeling. Walking ahead on the main level, down a few steps to the left, and threading through the corridor, one discovers a round structure where chemistry classes were once held, Croft Chapter House. It has been said that the room was designed this way to contain chemical explosions so they would blow the roof off rather than damage the rest of the building. Croft Chapter House is one of Toronto's most comfortable meeting spaces: high windows to let in light, a gently enfolding ceiling dome surmounted by a cupola over a circle of small clerestory windows. There are portraits on the walls, including one of Professor John Polanyi, who was awarded the Nobel prize for Chemistry in 1986.

Just outside Croft Chapter House is a stone porch. Where the porch roof meets the wall of Croft Chapter House is a carved head, claimed to be Ivan Reznikoff, who crafted many of the best carvings in

University College coat of arms, found in West Hall.

the building. Reznikoff and another stonemason, Diabolos, were apparently in love with the same woman. In mockery, Diabolos is said to have carved this as Reznikoff's likeness. The two fought in a vicious struggle throughout the building, and Reznikoff was fatally stabbed, Diabolos escaping into thin air. The head shows a much-demented man.

East from the central rotunda, the main floor hallway is panelled, with a plaster ceiling. It terminates in a large hallway at the southeast corner, where a carved newel post anchors the staircase leading up to the second floor. The wooden staircase continues upward in a spiral. North along the main floor corridor, remarkable carved columns frame glass that separates the hallway from the lecture rooms. The corridor leads to a wooden staircase with a long-admired carved newel post featuring a sleeping dragon. Climbing the stairs gives a view of the wooden ceiling over the stairwell, and through the windows, the quadrangle formed by the arms of the college, including the cloister on the west side. Originally student residences, the cloister now houses offices. The north side of the quadrangle is occupied by a plain, nondescript library designed by Mathers and Haldenby, built from 1963 to '64, and not in keeping with the rich detail of the original structure.

One special surprise is on the west side of the building, just to the north of the Croft Chapter House. Here, parts of the structure

"It is one of the chief virtues of the Gothic builders, that they never suffered ideas of outside symmetries and consistencies to interfere with the real use and value of what they did. If they wanted a window, they opened one; a room, they added one; a buttress, they built one; utterly regardless of any established conventionalities of external appearance, knowing (as indeed it always happened) that such daring interruptions of the formal plan would rather give additional interest to its symmetry than inure it. So that, in the best times of Gothic, a useless window would rather have been opened in an unexpected place for the sake of the surprise, than a useful one forbidden for the sake of symmetry."

—Ruskin continued, in his chapter "The Nature of Gothic"

gradually grow smaller and closer to the ground, until finally the roof of the house where the caretaker should live, at the extreme northwest corner of the complex, almost touches the ground. It is as though the whole structure has emerged from the earth at this particular juncture and erupted into marvels of construction.

The organic quality of this building, how it flows from one element to another with variety and surprise, its marvellous stone and wooden detail, its perspectives and views that unexpectedly emerge at staircases and doors all testify to Cumberland & Storm's ability to create the kind of Victorian Gothic environment that Ruskin wrote about so ardently. This is a building that is worth many, many visits, both to explore its interior and to view the exterior from different locations.

Army tents behind University College in 1914. The plane flying overhead is the Jenny JN4, built at Leaside (CTA 1244-752).

WOMEN'S ART ASSOCIATION OF CANADA

23 Prince Arthur Avenue

The Women's Art Association of Canada was formed in the late 1880s from a meeting between Lady Aberdeen, wife of the governor general, and the Toronto artist Mary Dignam. They agreed to create an organization that would help women become artists and improve their skills. In 1907 legislation was passed by Parliament that established the Association, and branches soon developed throughout the country. In 1916 the Association purchased these buildings, a pair of semi-detached, two-and-a-half-storey brick houses common in the latter decades of the nineteenth century, now melded into one structure.

The Association had a strong relationship in the 1920s with the Group of Seven and gave honorary membership to A. Y. Jackson and Arthur Lismer. Many of the most impressive Canadian women artists were involved with the Association: Emily Carr, Frances Loring, Florence Wyle, and Dorothy Stevens, and examples of their work are now found in the building. Workshops were offered for women and children, and once the public school system began to offer these technical art courses, the Association turned to supporting artists through scholarships and helping mature women maintain their interest in art and cultural activities. The Association established the first scholarship at the Ontario College of Art in 1947 and now provides them for other institutions like the National Ballet of Canada and the Royal Conservatory of Music. The Association runs a full program of lectures, exhibitions, and events relating to the arts, generally serving the needs of women.

Number 23 Prince Arthur was constructed in 1886 for a Yorkville merchant, and sometime later he added, as the other half of this pair of semi-detached houses, number 21 for his daughter and her husband. The main floors of the buildings have been merged into a single gallery and lecture space. One room on the main floor maintains the original Victorian atmosphere, as well as displaying art from the first half of the twentieth century and Association memorabilia. Studio space on the upper floors is rented out to artists.

This section of Prince Arthur Avenue has undergone considerable change in the past forty years. Some of the houses have been renovated for professional uses by lawyers and accountants, or for galleries and restaurants, so the primarily residential aspect of the street has disappeared. Directly across from the Association is one of the many high-rise buildings designed by Uno Prii, which, with its typical Toronto slab form and concrete struts, rises directly from the ground, showing little respect for the remnants of the nineteenth century that surround it.

ZEIDLER GRINNELL PARTNERSHIP

315 Queen Street West

The Zeidler Grinnell Partnership (formerly Zeidler Roberts) is one of the most well known and influential architectural firms in the city. It designed Ontario Place (now much altered) in the 1960s, the Eaton Centre in the mid-1970s, the renovation of the Queen's Quay Terminal Buildings in the 1980s, and the Rotman School of Management at the University of Toronto in the 1990s. One famous project outside Toronto is Vancouver's Canada Place, which has the appearance of incorporating the sails from a nineteenth-century schooner.

The firm's current home is at 315 Queen Street West, a structure it designed and built for its own use in the early 1980s, before Queen Street West had the cachet it has today. It is clearly designed to be on a main street—four storeys high, with the top storey angled back just a trifle to allow the sun to reach the sidewalk. The facade is post-modern, with its repeated square windows and the abbreviated concrete pillars between the shops. The comparatively undistinguished one- and two-storey buildings to the west demonstrate that main streets need and deserve more than small, modest buildings. Fortunately, the block on the north side of Queen has a form comparable to the Zeidler Grinnell building.

Inside are surprises. Architectural models are placed in the atrium around the curving staircase to the second level. There, the room opens unexpectedly into a large two-storey atrium comfortably filled with plants. The skylights were designed to provide much light into this space, but that was in an era before computers were customary in architectural firms. Today, designs are created on computers, and every architect works on one, which accounts for the many umbrellas in the workspaces around and in this atrium: they are needed to provide enough shade to make it possible to read what's on the screens.

A few dozen yards to the east, at John Street, is the Citytv building. This originally housed the printing presses of the Methodist Church (later United Church) of Canada, hence the open book among the detailing at the corners of the second-storey level. When it was built during the First World War, its steel framing and large windows put it in the forefront of Canadian architecture. The terra-cotta cladding and Gothic detailing, reminding one of the original religious origins, give it a great deal of visual appeal.

EAST

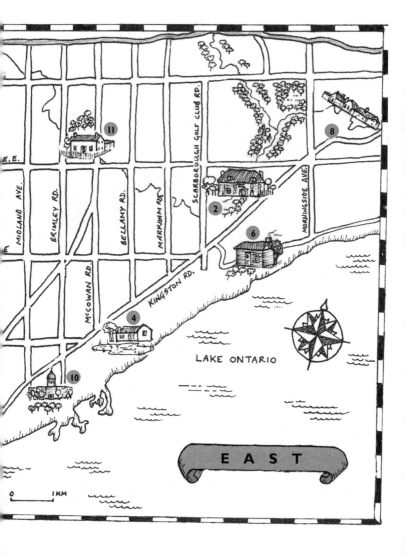

BEACH HEBREW INSTITUTE

109 Kenilworth Avenue

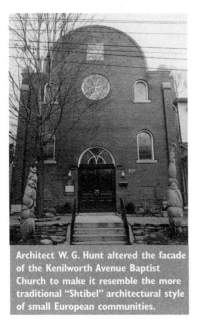

Architect W. G. Hunt altered the facade of the Kenilworth Avenue Baptist Church to make it resemble the more traditional "Shtibel" architectural style of small European communities.

This modest wood-and-brick building began life in 1895 as the **Kenilworth Avenue Baptist Church.** It faced onto Queen Street and had a steeply pitched roof with a small belfry. It obviously was successful in its function, for the church congregation grew so large that within a decade property was purchased for a new church on Waverley Road, just north of Queen.

Once the move to the new church was made, this building remained vacant for a few years, became a warehouse, then a community centre, and in 1920 it was purchased by the Beth Jacob Congregation to be used as a synagogue serving the Beach community. The building was subsequently moved several hundred feet south and rotated a quarter turn to face east. It now stands beside 107 Kenilworth Avenue, which had been the manse of the Baptist church.

Under the direction of the architect W. G. Hunt, the brick facade was added and altered to effect the congregation's idea of what a synagogue should look like: a semicircular parapet was placed at the top of the facade, with the Star of David affixed, and small arched windows were added to either side. (The rose window in the main facade survives from the Baptist church.)

The interior—it is small, and the dark colours contribute a formal element—was also changed to serve its new religious purposes. The ark is at the front of the sanctuary, with a table for the Torah before it. The room is devoid of decoration, its drama coming from the simplicity of the dark wood of the pews, table, ark, and ceiling beams against the white walls. Marble plaques in the entrance and sanctuary record the names of the founders of the synagogue. There is a small balcony, added by Hunt, for women.

Over the years the congregation has ebbed and flowed in size, and for the past few decades has been undergoing something of a revival, currently with membership of 130 families. Many think of the Beach community as homogenously Christian and white, but resources such as this make it clear that here, as in Toronto generally, diversity predominates.

The modest size of the building seems entirely appropriate for a street of homes mostly built as cottages, and over time expanded, giving each a shape that seems organic in nature. Compared with the huge new homes on the old racetrack just west of Woodbine, the buildings on Kenilworth might be thought to be too small and too cramped. But as the residents will tell you, a small footprint is entirely appropriate for most households today.

CEDAR RIDGE CREATIVE CENTRE

225 Confederation Drive

Cedar Ridge is a handsome house—once known as Uplands—built in the years just before the First World War, on a high cliff overlooking Highland Creek. To the south lies the Scarborough Golf and Country Club, and were it not for the dense growth of trees on the north bank of the creek, the south porch of the house would provide a magnificent view of those playing on the links.

Both the golf club and this property were purchased as one parcel by Charles C. Cummings in 1911. R. Nicholls was retained to design a large house in the Arts and Crafts style of the day, making abundant use of dressed oak, particularly noticeable in the main entrance and stairway. The built-in buffet in the dining room remains, and in the middle of the floor is a buzzer that could be pressed to summon servants. Several other structures on the property were designed by Nicholls, including a gardener's cottage, a stable (considered the carriage house), and a garage. A building of similar design to the main house was created for the golf club.

The financier John Fraser purchased the mansion in 1927 and renamed it Cedar Ridge. The gardens he developed were impressive enough to be featured in *Canadian Homes and Gardens* magazine in 1942, and much of their charm is still apparent.

Many decades later, the property was purchased by Metro Toronto for a regional park. Surrounding residents who had moved into the suburban homes built around Cedar Ridge in the 1960s opposed Metro's plans for an active park with ball diamonds and wading pool, apparently fearing the intrusion of large crowds. In response, the City of Scarborough encouraged the buildings to be used for local art programs, which explains current cultural activity. For a decade the City relied on volunteers, then in 1985 began operating its programs directly. Today the large main floor rooms of the house are display space, the Cedar Ridge Gallery, usually exhibiting local artists, and the upper floor has become studios and classrooms for pottery, fibre art, woodcarving, and other artistic pursuits. The Ontario Clay and Glass Association occupies the cottage. Since the creation of the megacity in 1998, funds for endeavours like Cedar Ridge have been limited, and the programs appear to be at considerable risk. One hopes Cedar Ridge can stand as a good model for local government support of arts, heritage, and a local community.

The Cedar Ridge Creative Centre was originally a fourteen-room summer home for Charles C. Cummings's family. It was completed in 1912–13.

DON JAIL

The Don Jail opened in 1865. It is shown here in 1930 (CTA 1244-1152).

🏛 550 Gerrard Street East (at Don Jail Roadway)

By the middle of the 1800s when the city's jail at Front and Parliament Streets was deemed too small and decrepit, the city fathers looked for a large site more amenable to the rehabilitation of prisoners. They chose a rising knoll on the east side of the Don River in the midst of a large market garden.

William Thomas, an architect originally from England, who had recently completed St. Lawrence Hall, was retained. His design was based on the latest prison thinking of the day, namely, the panopticon—a series of cell blocks radiating out from a central guard station, from where many prisoners could be viewed. Thomas designed four cell blocks, but only two were built.

The principal block is the most interesting. Its main entrance is presided over by a fearsome bearded face intended to strike terror into the hearts of those entering through the massive doors. Sturdy columns on either side, with their bands of stone vermiculation (carving in shapes that resemble worms), seem bound with cords, perhaps reflecting on the state of many prisoners. The windows are small and the block has heavy corner treatment, all giving the jail a deliberately ominous presence. Its looming aspect probably led many people to suggest, from the mid-twentieth century on, that the building should be demolished.

Inside is a gloomy semi-circular space rising three high storeys to a half-octagonal skylight. Walkways, which ring the upper floors, are supported by iron brackets on which serpents and gargoyles sport. It is said that floggings took place in this central location for all other prisoners to hear—a worrisome way to teach by example. The governor (as wardens were then called) and his family lived in a suite in the jail for some time but eventually moved into the modest house directly south at 558 Gerrard Street, perhaps hoping to establish some distance between home life and the screams of inmate suffering. The house is now used for programs helping former inmates and those prisoners ready to be integrated back into the community.

The cells are plain and tiny, although in terms of space per prisoner, not wildly different from the overcrowded conditions that can be found in the new jail facility next door. In the daytime, prisoners were expected to mingle and exercise in the corridors (rather than spending virtually all their time in cells). One section of the jail, Number 9 Hospital, was at first an infirmary, but was later subdivided into four self-contained units, slightly larger than the standard cells. Since inmates of these cells were rarely permitted to leave them, there was less supervision, which led to the escape in September 1952 of the notorious Boyd Gang.

Edwin Alonzo Boyd was a man with Erroll Flynn looks, and starting in 1949 he showed a penchant for robbing banks. Two years later, in mid-October, he was apprehended and placed in the Don Jail, awaiting trial. In November 1951 he and two gang members, Leonard Jackson and Willie Jackson (not related), escaped from the corridor that fronted their cells by sawing through bars using a file carefully hidden in Leonard's artificial foot. The gang continued its spree, robbing local banks and making off with the very large sum of $46,270 from a bank in Leaside. In March 1952, Leonard Jackson and gang member Steve Suchan shot police sergeant Edmund Tong, who died several weeks later. After a brief but intensive manhunt, the gang was again incarcerated, and again, on September 8, 1952, they escaped—this time through the bars of Number 9 Hospital, using a saw smuggled in by a friendly lawyer and a makeshift key they had fashioned with a file. A massive manhunt ensued, and the gang was finally captured in a barn in North York. Suchan and Leonard Jackson were convicted and sentenced to hang: they died, back to back, at a double hanging in the jail on December 16, 1952.

The rotunda.

Boyd served a long sentence and then was given a new identity and moved to western Canada. About seventy hangings took place in the jail—the last, a double one in 1962—before capital punishment fell from use and then was prohibited in

Canada in the 1970s. Thomas's jail has not housed prisoners since 1977.

In the 1960s, the east wing was partially demolished in order to make space for the mean and unpleasant-looking jail that still stands. The red-brick structure is crowded, a result perhaps of the general closing of mental institutions in the 1970s, since today about half of the inmates here suffer from mental illness. For many years the old Don Jail has remained vacant while people have wondered what to do with it. Now Riverdale Hospital, which is behind the jail in a modern semi-circular structure, may revive the

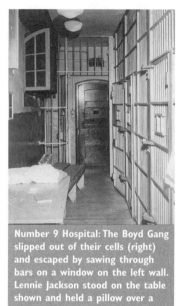

Number 9 Hospital: The Boyd Gang slipped out of their cells (right) and escaped by sawing through bars on a window on the left wall. Lennie Jackson stood on the table shown and held a pillow over a microphone in the ceiling.

building. After being ordered in 1998 by the provincial government to close and relocate its three hundred plus residents, the hospital successfully argued that its role, focusing on rehabilitation and long-term care, was critical to the health care system. The province has agreed that it should not only remain open but also has provided it with funds to purchase the jail property and expand onto it. One wonders whether any kind of rehabilitation will overcome the "ominous atmosphere" that seems to have stuck with Thomas's original design.

Not only will the old jail be renovated, but the province has announced that the newer red-brick jail will be closed. That raises the question of the location of jail facilities. This downtown jail provides easy access by family members to prisoners, which a suburban location could not do. What's more, for all its notoriety, the jail's existence has never been challenged by the many urbane residents of the adjacent Riverdale area, whereas a new facility would be sure to stir up a storm in virtually any neighbourhood. Perhaps there is a strong argument for replacing the red-brick facility with a contemporary equivalent of Thomas's mid-nineteenth-century masterpiece.

FOOL'S PARADISE
(HOME OF THE ARTIST DORIS McCARTHY)

1 Meadowcliffe Drive

Doris McCarthy was born in Toronto in 1910, and her interest in art led to a scholarship to the Ontario College of Art, where she studied with the Group of Seven artists Arthur Lismer and J. E. H. MacDonald. Early in the 1930s, she began teaching at Central Technical School with the Toronto Board of Education, a position she held for forty years.

McCarthy possesses much of the rebel talent often found in artists, and in looking for a place to call home in the late 1930s, she discovered this property, a tiny bit of pasture at the bottom of a hill, sitting on the edge of the Scarborough Bluffs, in a remote corner of the district. She began camping here in a tent. In 1939 she purchased the property, naming it Fool's Paradise, as her mother considered the property beyond her means. During the Second World War, the beginnings of a house took shape, but a labour shortage meant she had a hand in building it, including pouring the concrete liner for her fifty-two-foot-deep well. The house was largely completed by the end of the war, when McCarthy moved in, although it was without electricity, given the isolated nature of the property.

To travel between the city and Fool's Paradise, McCarthy purchased a jeep, for which she became renowned. One friend addressed a letter to "The girl with the jeep, Scarborough," and the post office delivered it to her. (That's a story she tells in the first volume of her autobiography,

A Fool's Paradise.) McCarthy has continued to occupy the property, and suburbia has made its way virtually to her door. Nevertheless, one admires the continued remote quality of the property, the serenity of the reflecting pond, and that the lawn proceeds to the very edge of the Bluffs, which plummet sixty-five to a hundred feet into the lake.

The two-bedroom house is an affectionate collection of additions and has the nice rambling feeling of having been lived in well. In 1999 McCarthy donated the property to the Ontario Heritage Foundation, with a generous maintenance endowment. Once she moves out, it will be available for artists to use as a retreat.

Doris McCarthy has created an extraordinary artistic career that continues well past her ninetieth year. Many examples of her work are found throughout her home. McCarthy has won numerous awards and has played a role in almost every serious art organization in Canada. She was named a Member of the Order of Canada in 1986 and currently exhibits through the Wynick Tuck Gallery at 401 Richmond Street West.

This one-storey frame house on the Scarborough Bluffs has been the artist's home and studio since 1940.

GOULDING ESTATE

305 Dawes Road

In the early decades of the twentieth century, the Massey family owned Dentonia Park Farm, a large chunk of land on either side of Taylor Creek. The farm included a magnificent four-storey barn, since demolished, located on the south bank of the creek, just east of Dawes Road. Urban development has since consumed much of the farm property, save for Taylor Bush Park, established on either side of the stream, and 305 Dawes Road.

Dorothy Massey and her husband, Dr. Goulding, built this house in 1921 to have a view of the barn across the valley. It is done in comfortable Arts and Craft style, with leaded windows and natural wood detailing, including, in the pantry, a splendid large wooden cupboard with glass doors, simple enough to seem to have come from the Shaker era of the late eighteenth century. The living room is spacious and wide, set down a few steps from the rest of the house to make it seem linked directly with the earth. The basement was an important rehearsal space for the Toronto Children's Players, an organization Dorothy Massey founded and then supported for twenty-five years. The grounds include a dry stone wall, a small decorative pool, and areas covered with flagstone. Natural growth around the building provides a real sense of isolation from the nearby city.

In the 1960s the property was purchased by a developer, and the building was threatened with demolition. The Borough of East York expropriated the property to protect it. For some years the house was used as a group home for young teenagers, then it remained vacant for a while, and recently has been rented from the city by the Centre for Creative Ministries, which has a mission "to promote compassionate leadership for adults seeking to live their lives in more meaningful ways for themselves and their communities." Various programs are offered, including yoga. The Centre has also rekindled interest in children's theatre, with a children's Peace Theatre. In 2000 the Centre held the first reunion since 1955 of the Toronto Children's Players.

THE GUILD
(FORMERLY THE GUILD OF ALL ARTS)

191 Guildwood Parkway

In 1914 a retired American general named Harold Bickford built his country home, Ranelagh Park, on this land. Seven years later, he sold the property to the Foreign Missionary of the Roman Catholic Church, which subsequently moved close to St. Augustine's Seminary farther east along Kingston Road. In 1932, in the depths of the Depression,

The Guild Inn.

A keystone from what was once a doorway of the Bank of Toronto.

the property was purchased by Rosa Breithaupt Hewetson, a young widow with four children, just prior to her marriage to Spencer Clark. Rosa was a talented pianist, Spencer an electrical engineer with an interest in cultural and architectural heritage. Together they created the Guild of All Arts, with the objective of supporting crafts and decorative arts (known as the Arts and Crafts movement) as advocated by the late-nineteenth-century English designer and thinker William Morris.

Under the Clarks' tutelage, the Bickford House was added to and expanded, so the original building is not readily apparent. Workshops and studios were established for an array of craft activity in outbuildings on the estate. The Earl Greys Players—an early group that produced Shakespeare plays in Toronto—rehearsed here, and Sir Ernest Macmillan and the Hambourg brothers (Clem ran the famous jazz club on Grenville Street in the 1950s, House of Hambourg) rehearsed and composed here. Bickford's stable became the Studio, a workshop for artisans. Another building became a sculpture studio. A log cabin dating from the 1850s was maintained.

During the Second World War, the Canadian government used the property as a training facility for the Women's Royal Naval Service (WRENS) and as a hospital for shell-shocked soldiers. When the Clarks returned to their home after the war, the guild idea had passed, and they turned their interest—it continued to 1981—to operating a hotel and rescuing fragments of buildings being demolished in the city and environs, creating a veritable boneyard of important historical buildings. Here can be found remnants of what the city has lost by refusing to protect its historic structures. We have the Clarks to thank for reminding us of the vital role that we play in safeguarding the heritage left to us.

At the entrance to the property is a four-sided bas-relief showing representations of four Canadian provinces. On other parts of the property are the remaining panels, representing, in all, the ten provinces and two territories. These carvings were created for the Bank of Montreal, on the northwest corner of King and Bay Streets, which was begun in 1939, delayed by the war, completed in 1948, and demolished in 1972. They are works by the finest artists in Toronto at the time—Emanuel Hahn, Frances Loring, Florence Wyle, Elizabeth Wyn Wood, Donald Stewart, and Jacobine Jones.

On the grounds at the rear of the house are the columns and archways from the elegant Bank of Toronto, demolished to make way for the Toronto–Dominion Centre. There are the Art Deco panels that graced the former *Toronto Star* building at 80 King Street West; the moose head and other pieces from the main entrance to the Temple Building once on Bay Street at Queen; a gateway formed from the turrets of the Produce Exchange Building once at Scott and Colborne Streets; and many other items of great interest.

The whole of the property was sold to the metropolitan and provincial governments in 1978 and is now managed by the City. Arrangements have been made for a new hotel operator to take over the structures and create an economically viable hotel facility, with the building graveyard continuing to be managed by the City's parks department.

The Guild Inn Amphitheatre is the centrepiece of the Sculpture Park. It was reconstructed by Clifford Restoration Limited from the salvaged columns of the Bank of Toronto (shown on page 93), which once stood at the corner of King and Bay Streets.

GURDWARA SHROMANI SIKH SANGAT

269 Pape Avenue

The first Sikh temple in Toronto.

The first Sikhs came to Canada as part of a military group from Hong Kong to celebrate the coronation of King Edward VII in 1902. Almost four thousand Sikhs settled in British Columbia, establishing their first *gurdwara*, or temple, there in 1908, the year when in a burst of racism Canadian law prevented further immigration by Sikhs.

In 1920 wives and children were permitted to join Sikh men, but immigration policies did not become more liberal until the 1950s. The decades-old tradition of this community in the West explains the successful push in the 1980s to permit Sikh members of the Royal Canadian Mounted Police to wear traditional turbans.

Established in 1969, Gurdwara Shromani Sikh Sangat is the first Sikh temple in Toronto, which says something about the time involved in the community moving across the country from the West Coast. Gurdwaras are community based and self-governing, each temple pursuing its own practices, determined by community preferences. The Sikh religion is monotheistic, combining Hindu and Islamic elements, and was founded in India's Punjab region by Guru Nanak in the sixteenth century.

This temple was established as a centre of Sikh worship in Toronto but has since been superseded by much larger and more wealthy temples in Mississauga and York Region. The current congregation is small. The building was originally an industrial structure, and the adaptations made are not significant. The kitchen and eating area (Sunday services are followed by a meal) occupies most of the main floor. On the upper level is the large open room that serves as the main place of worship, with the holy book, Guru Granth Sahib, resting in the altar-like structure at the head of the room, among a profusion of coloured textiles.

MILLER LASH HOUSE

130 Old Kingston Road
(Scarborough Campus, University of Toronto)

Miller Lash was a wealthy Toronto businessman, and the story goes that in 1913, on a Sunday drive in his chauffeur-driven Stanley Steamer car, he found himself on Old Kingston Road in the Highland Creek Valley. The stream was amply filled with water, the forest was thick and the meadows lush, and Lash decided to buy the site as his country estate.

The American architect Edward B. Green designed a sprawling single-storey house in the Arts and Crafts style popular in the first two decades of the twentieth century—it emphasized simple wood finishes, white plaster, and subdued the intrusion of technology.

This house looks west through the Highland Creek valley. It is one of Toronto's first poured-concrete houses, and stone from the river has been embedded to give a rough and ready feel to the exterior. The roof over-hang is large, and inside the building the squared pine wooden rafters—likely milled on the property—rise to cathedral ceilings. Both floor and roof are covered in terra-cotta tile. Wood-framed windows and French doors—both since removed—opened directly onto the patio, blurring the distinction between interior and exterior. Three skylights bring a flood of natural light into the interior hallway running the length of

A side view of the house.

the building. It is an expansive and welcoming home, replete with five fireplaces, and sits confidently in the valley.

Lash died in 1942, and the next owner sold the property to the University of Toronto in 1963 when the Scarborough Campus was established to the northeast across Highland Creek. The house served as the residence of the first principals of Scarborough College, although that brief tradition ended in 1976. The building was designated a heritage property in 1998, and the university is gathering funds to restore it. The grounds are actively used for recreation purposes. Visitors should not miss the opportunity, after viewing the house, to walk down by the Highland Creek.

Miller Lash should not be confused with Lash Miller, a professor of chemistry at University of Toronto for almost four decades in the first half of the twentieth century, after whom the Lash Miller Chemistry building on St. George Street is named.

R. C. HARRIS FILTRATION PLANT

2701 Queen Street East

The Filtration Plant is one of the great mythic buildings in Toronto. It is a surprise on first viewing and remains in the imagination for a long time. Perhaps this strong impression is created

The R. C. Harris Filtration Plant is Toronto's finest complex of Art Deco buildings and one of Canada's most extraordinary public works.

A view of some of the many settling beds, where much of Toronto's water is purified.

by the utter flatness of the lawn (under which are settling beds), or the symmetry, length, and grandeur of the main building, or the handsome entrance looking over the lake. Some call it the "Palace of Purification." It has been featured in Canadian art; Michael Ondaatje wrote compellingly about it in his novel *In the Skin of a Lion*.

The building was designed by Thomas Pomphrey in 1930. (He also designed the Cenotaph in front of Old City Hall.) The western half was built in the 1930s to provide jobs in the Depression; the eastern half (the filter building) was constructed in the 1950s, as demand for water in the expanding city grew. The plant currently processes and pumps about 175 million gallons of water a day, supplying almost half the water needs of the City of Toronto and York Region. The water intake pipes are 1½ miles from shore. The raw water is pre-chlorinated, screened, and alum is added to capture impurities, which are removed in settling beds; it is then filtrated, post-chlorinated, and fluoridated before distribution. Quality testing occurs about eight times a day. The importance of this complex—both in function and design—has led to its declaration as a National Historic Civil Engineering Site. A large pumphouse on the lake side of the complex has enough external

In his novel In the Skin of a Lion, Michael Ondaatje describes R. C. Harris's concern the night Patrick Lewis swims through the lake intakes into the filtration plant carrying dynamite:

"Harris, half asleep on the makeshift bed in his office, has heard the thump, one thump that didn't fit into the pattern made by the row of water pumps. He walks onto the mezzanine of the pumping station. It is brilliantly lit and stark. In his dressing gown he descends the stairs to the low-level pumping station, walks twenty-five yards into the Venturi tunnels, and then returns slowly, listening again for that false thump. He has seen nothing but the grey-painted machines."

Inside the pumphouse, where water is drawn in from Lake Ontario.

detailing to function in some people's minds as a religious building. Inside are dozens of large pumps drawing the raw water from the lake and pumping the finished water into the city's distribution pipes.

A good place to begin a tour is at the main doors on the south side. The entrance is in a block set slightly forward, through a tall arch, flanked by towers. Both the stonework and the small windows give the building a slight look of a mausoleum. The motif of the broken arch—the intrusion in the curve of the arch renders it weak—is repeated in the many windows across the filtration wings.

Inside is extraordinary marble and travertine on the floors and walls and fittings of bronze and chrome, all in grand Art Deco style. The main rotunda has a tower clock and assorted equipment to monitor the progress of the water from lake bottom to drinking glass. The wings leading to the filtration pools are lit by peaked skylights and feel exceptionally airy and clean. There is a heroic quality to these spaces, although the doors to the filter beds open to a more dubious world— a large dark field of watery pools, the concrete edges dank and wet, the ceiling low, the air cool and liquid. This is a different kind of magic.

The plant was named in 1946 after Rowland Caldwell Harris, commissioner of Public Works for Toronto from 1912 to 1945, when he died. Harris had led a major program of public works construction in the 1920s and '30s, including the Bloor Street Viaduct over the Don Valley and the remarkable yellow brick and banded-stone public works buildings sprinkled throughout the former City of Toronto (such as on Richmond Street, west of Spadina). They define the importance of well-designed structures to give the public realm of the city character and definition.

The rotunda, the tower clock presides over the purification systems.

ST. AUGUSTINE'S SEMINARY OF TORONTO

 2661 Kingston Road

It must have been a remarkable sight for early-twentieth-century travellers to come across the dome of St. Augustine's Seminary floating high above the empty fields of Scarborough. Even today, after suburbia has encroached almost up to the footings of the building, the dome has a mysterious presence.

In 1910 construction of St. Augustine's started, to the design of A. W. Holmes, and the seminary, the first for English-speaking Roman Catholics in Canada, was dedicated in 1913. The seminary consists of dormitories, offices, lecture rooms, a library, and a chapel, all simply done in stone at the main level and brick above. The porch, with its steps and columns, provides the only hint that there are delights within.

Inside, the foyer, displaying several portraits of religious leaders of the seminary, opens to a broad rotunda and halls to either side. Ahead are the doors to the chapel, which is decorated in the Italian style with frescoes on the ceiling, the Stations of the Cross, and small sculptures on the side walls. The chapel has an intense and formal quality that is something of a surprise outside a city centre. Above is the glorious tower, designed to cool the building. As originally constructed, the central rotunda opened directly to the dome, and when the windows in the clerestory under the dome were open, air would be drawn upward, thus cooling the main structure. An intervening floor has since been added, and the dome's main function now is to be alluring. Sadly, it is not open to the public. One can imagine the views overlooking the remaining acreage, to the lip of the bluffs, but a hundred yards away.

With the declining interest in the priesthood in Canada, the seminary now attracts students of the priesthood from throughout the world.

SCARBOROUGH HISTORICAL MUSEUM

1007 Brimley Road

David Thomson, Scarborough's first non-aboriginal resident, arrived in Upper Canada in 1796 and settled on this piece of land; his home is thought to have been on what is now St. Andrew's Road, which runs along the northeast side of the park.

He and his brother Andrew were stonemasons (they worked on the first Parliament buildings at Front and Parliament Streets) and had a farm here. Highland Creek, which flows through the property, was then a substantial stream and brimmed with salmon. Since then, this creek—like other water courses in the city—has generally been starved for rainwater, which is piped to the lake rather than allowed to filter into the ground and ensure a high water table.

When the area north of Lawrence Avenue was being developed for a suburban subdivision in the 1960s, the remaining members of the Thomson family agreed to sell a good chunk of land to the city at a very reasonable price, permitting the Thomson Memorial Park to be established. Just at that time, the Cornell House, built in 1858 at

The Scarborough Historical Museum buildings portray various periods in Scarborough's past.

Markham and Eglinton, was threatened with demolition. Scarborough Council responded in the same way too many councils do: rather than agreeing to protect historical artifacts as found and building to accommodate them, Council decided to move the house here. Since one historical building is thought to look forlorn, others were relocated to keep it company—a log house and two smaller structures. Fortunately, the ingenuity of heritage staff has made a pleasant and cohesive display of these movable bits of history.

The Cornell House, with its white clapboard and green trim, is in the vernacular style common to Upper Canada. This simple housing form was copiously copied by Wartime Housing Limited, the federal government's housing provider right after the Second World War, although of the fifty thousand similar structures built throughout the country, few remain. (Several examples can be found on the southern reaches of Royal York Road in Etobicoke.) The building was originally the home of Charles and Matilda Cornell and their eight children, and family members lived in it until the early decades of the twentieth century. Further historical continuity was provided through Albert Campbell, the mayor of Scarborough at the time the Thomson Park was established—he was married to a descendant of the Cornell family. Today, the building is furnished in a style of the period just before the Great War.

There were many connections between families in the early city. The father of Charles C. Cornell, William, was a widower when he married his second wife, Rhoda Terry. She was the widow of Parshall Terry, a man who invested in what is now known as Todmorden Mills. Both William and Rhoda brought their own children to the marriage, and between them they produced another half-dozen—in all, they were responsible for a total of thirty-seven children.

Immediately to the rear is a small white structure, the Kennedy Discovery Gallery, now an activity centre, with flooring and wainscotting taken from the Methodist Church in the Malvern community before its demolition in 1976. The McCowan Log House, moved here from the banks of Wilcott Creek in northeast Scarborough, has been handsomely restored to its 1850 style. The fourth building is a representation of a carriage works, with a display of the tools used in Hough Carriage Works, which stood at Eglinton Avenue and Birchmount Road.

TODMORDEN MILLS HERITAGE MUSEUM AND ARTS CENTRE

🏛 Pottery Road

The Terry house.

I n 1794, when the Town of York had about two hundred residents, the Skinner brothers, Isaiah and Aaron, began construction of the first mill on the Don River. Lumber sawn here was purchased by Lieutenant-Governor John Graves Simcoe and his wife, Elizabeth, to build their summer home, Castle Frank, on the west bank of the Don just south of where the Bloor Street Viaduct is now located. Elizabeth made a small sketch of the mill as it was in 1796, beside a then-sizable river that carried large rafts of logs to the mill and produced abundant fish. Several years later, Simcoe agreed that the Skinners could add a grist mill to produce flour (the lieutenant-governor was invested with significant power). This little hive of industry became known as Don Mills. Parshall Terry invested in the mills before drowning in the Don River in July 1808 while attempting to ford it on his horse.

Thomas Helliwell's 1838 residence.

In 1821 new investors entered the picture—John Eastwood and Thomas Helliwell. The Helliwell Brewery opened in 1821 on the site of Don Mills, which Helliwell renamed Todmorden after the English town he came from. The brewery operated until 1847. For his part, John Eastwood took up the government's challenge, suggested by William Lyon Mackenzie, to establish the first paper mill in Upper Canada. He nearly made it; Eastwood's mill opened in 1827, eight months after the first near Hamilton.

Beginning in 1830, Mackenzie purchased paper from Eastwood for the publication of the *Colonial Advocate*. Eastwood later became a member of Toronto City Council, and joined the rebel cause in the Rebellion of 1837.

Several buildings on the site date from this period. The museum—as excellent and enchanting a local museum as one might expect to find—is located in a building sitting on the foundations of the brewery. The large, distinctive smokestack is from Eastwood's paper mill, currently undergoing restoration. Helliwell's house remains where it was built in 1838, a grey stucco building with wide eaves to protect the rare (unfired) adobe brick walls from rain. The interior has been furnished in the style of the 1860s. The yellow wooden clapboard Terry house was probably built a decade or more after the death of Parshall Terry in 1808. It has wide painted pine floorboards and is furnished in the style of the 1830s.

The Don River that powered the mill was diverted in the 1960s for the building of the Don Valley Expressway, which

John Eastwood's paper mill, with its landmark smoke stack.

too often fills this most historic of sites with noise and exhaust. One portion of the original course of the river can be found below the bridge just to the south of the buildings, before the main parking lot, where but a thin trickle of water remains to be seen. Slightly to the north is another historic site—the Don Valley Brick Works.

It is heartening to see such a collection of original buildings with significant stories to tell of the early history of Toronto. But political leaders have burdened the site with structures that don't belong—a train station moved north from Queen Street in 1969, which still, after more than three decades, looks quite out of place, and a washroom facility on the other side of the road shaped like—of all things—a Chinese pagoda.

NORTH

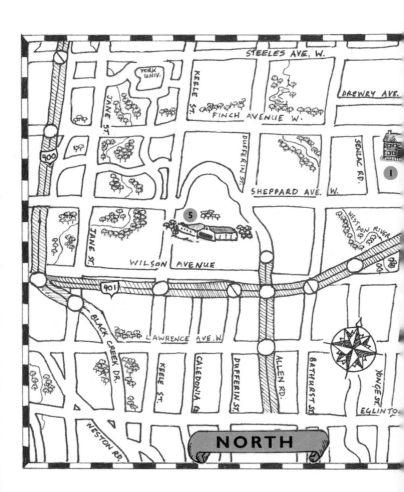

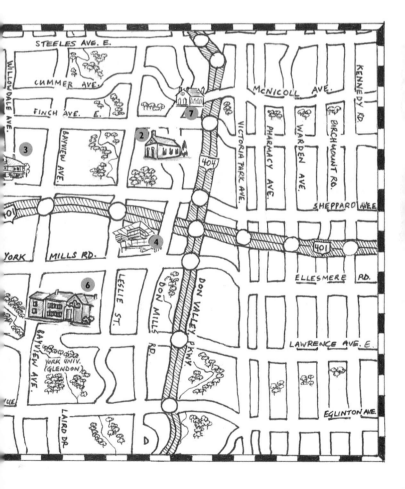

GIBSON HOUSE MUSEUM

 5172 Yonge Street

This earliest known photo of Gibson House, taken circa 1873, shows Eliza Milne Gibson, possibly in mourning, with her children and grandchildren on the front porch.

David Gibson was born in Arnefoyl, a small hamlet outside of Dundee, Scotland, in the early years of the nineteenth century and came to Upper Canada in 1829. He established his home on this land in a frame house, with his American-born wife, Eliza, and began a farm as an addition to his work as a surveyor.

William Lyon Mackenzie, a fellow Scot from Dundee, was the most active politically progressive voice in Upper Canada and attracted Gibson to join the cause. Gibson was elected to the Legislative Assembly in 1834 and was part of the small group planning the uprising in December 1837. When fellow rebel John Rolph wanted to get word to Mackenzie, who was visiting supporters in the area north of Toronto, he sent a messenger to Gibson's house.

Rolph's message was that the Lieutenant-Governor Francis Bond Head had learned of the uprising and that the proposed march on the city should be moved ahead from December 6 to December 4. The proposal was delivered on Saturday, December 2, and as word of it spread, it caused considerable consternation: given the time taken for communication and travel, it was difficult for those planning to gather at Montgomery's Tavern (on Yonge just north of Eglinton) on December 6 to arrive two days early. Mackenzie learned of the change only when he arrived at Gibson's on Sunday, December 3. The confusion proved fatal, as the rebels were never able to sufficiently organize their resources or set their strategy.

Like other rebel leaders, Gibson went into hiding after the failed insurgency and fled to United States. His house was set afire by government troops and severely damaged. He (like most other rebel leaders except Mackenzie) was pardoned in 1843 while in exile in the States, but since he had found work there as a surveyor, he did not return to Upper Canada until 1848. Fortunately, he had not been stripped of his properties—which perhaps is reflective of the general support in Upper Canada for the rebel aims.

In 1851 he built the house that still stands here. It is a two-storey Georgian-style one similar to Justice William Campbell's house and the Grange, with a tail for the kitchen at the rear. The rooms are spacious, particularly the living and dining rooms, which appear able to easily accommodate a grand feast or dance party. David and Eliza Gibson had seven children when they moved in, and the upstairs would have provided plenty of space for everyone.

The home is decorated in the style of the 1850s, and the painted pattern on the floor of the front foyer duplicates the choices of Gibson and his wife, as does the carefully painted "graniting" of the walls of the central hallway. The piano and other furnishings reflect the prosperity of the Gibson family. Income from surveying was supplemented by a farm that experimented in new styles of crops and farming methods. One vegetable grown here was mangel-wurzel, a large turnip used for horse feed.

The house remained in the Gibson family until the 1920s. It changed hands several times in the decades that followed, and in the late 1950s it was used as a boarding house. A decade later it fell vacant, was purchased by a developer, and its density rights were transferred to the property to the north to permit the construction of the apartment building that overlooks the house. The property was deeded to the then City of North York, which established the museum in Gibson House to give contemporary audiences a view into the city's past.

One of the more innovative programs run here is offered to immigrant students taking English as a Second Language courses. They cook a meal over the kitchen fire, 1850s-style, recognizing that they are following Gibson's footsteps: like them, Gibson was an immigrant to this country, trying to make a new life for himself.

HISTORIC ZION SCHOOLHOUSE

1091 Finch Avenue East

Miss Nellie Galbraith's class, in front of Zion School S.S. #12, circa 1918.

This one-room red-brick schoolhouse was built in 1869 to serve the surrounding farming community. By then public education, paid for by government, had been a reality in Upper Canada for almost two decades for both boys and girls up to their teenage years.

The style was typical of such structures built in the province: one room, a simple peaked roof, large windows to admit abundant light, a small cloakroom, and a place for a stove to provide heat. There would have been an outhouse. Most likely the teacher was a young single woman who boarded with a local farming family. Most students walked to school, and since farms were several hundred acres in size, no more than a few dozen children would be in the catchment area. The school offered comprehensive education to all grades in the one room, the older kids helping the younger, with an emphasis on the important skills of reading and arithmetic, as well as the social skills of co-operation and teamwork.

With the coming of suburban development in the 1950s, students were placed in classes of their own age in larger schools, and this building was closed in 1955. It was vacant for several decades, until former students—including one who had become a chief of police—undertook to save and restore the structure. The furniture, books, maps, and pictures on the wall harken to the era just before the First World War. (Visitors should note the map with the British Empire shown in pink.) Today students from larger schools visit to get a first-hand demonstration of education a century ago.

JOHN McKENZIE HOUSE
(ONTARIO HISTORICAL SOCIETY)

34 Parkview Avenue

John McKenzie was a successful farmer, working his late father's farm on land originally deeded to Jacob Cummer in 1801, when he decided in 1912 to sell a portion of his land for **house lots.** With the proceeds he built a grand home for his wife, Eva, and their family. The house lots were known as the Empress Subdivision, and they have become today's Willowdale community to the east of the John McKenzie house.

Construction of the new house began in 1913, and McKenzie reputedly spent $50,000, an enormous sum equal to perhaps twenty times that in today's value. It is an impressive three storeys of red brick, facing south, with a wide stone veranda supported by fluted stone columns wrapping around the front and east side. On the third floor are emphatic dormers. The front door is broad, framed by bevelled-glass panels leaded in an Art Nouveau pattern. The front hall is wide and panelled in white oak. Approaching the staircase, one can glimpse

John McKenzie House today, after restoration by the Ontario Historical Society for their headquarters.

on the second floor landing an attractive stained-glass window with flower motifs. The rooms on the main floor are panelled in the same white oak, and the floor is the original hardwood. The twelve-room house is comfortable and attractive without flamboyance. One wonders where the McKenzies, of farming stock in the midst of a farming community with little sophistication, found the inspiration to create such an elegant building.

In the rear yard, the 1907 brick Milk House—McKenzie's farm specialized in Holstein cattle—has been rebuilt on the original foun-

John and Eva McKenzie on the porch of their home.

dations, and the stable, dating to about 1915, has been renovated. The 1918 coach house has been rehabilitated and its doors carefully reconstructed according to old photographs.

The house remained in the McKenzie family until 1976, when it was sold to North York in exchange for air rights transferred to the massive apartment structures to the west. The City let the building stay abandoned for some years until Council agreed to lease the property to the Ontario

Historical Society—a public sector organization that focuses on provincial heritage issues—as its headquarters. The OHS raised the $500,000 needed for affectionate restoration and has hung a portrait of John Graves Simcoe, the first lieutenant-governor of Upper Canada, over the fireplace in the living room.

The neighbourhood has clearly changed since McKenzie's day. Parkview Avenue has been terminated to allow a ring road to be built. On one side is the new high-rise community linked to the North York downtown, and on the other, the older Willowdale neighbourhood. An unhappy tension of urban modes has been created, instead of a gradual change that could have enhanced the environs of McKenzie's fine legacy.

ONTARIO ASSOCIATION OF ARCHITECTS

111 Moatfield Drive

When the OAA found that its jewel of a Modernist building at 50 Park Road was no longer big enough to meet its needs, it decided on a suburban site, then held a design competition among its members, the process used to build 50 Park Road. The winner was Ruth Cawker, a young Toronto architect, and her building has been the subject of much discussion in the profession ever since.

The building is on a lot wedged between a nineteenth-century brick farmhouse (moved, in the suburban style, to this location in the 1980s to protect it from demolition) and a rather clunky Modernist office building. It sits on stilts to provide parking directly under the structure, and visitors walk up an impressive staircase giving views

across a small valley to Don Mills Road and the larger valley beyond. The building is light and almost transparent. The main level is a two-storey glass hall, from which lead passages to a display area, a conference centre, a lounge, and offices. There are walkways at the level above to provide views down to the atrium and more small meeting rooms. On the roof are open metal louvres.

Writing in the magazine *Canadian Architect* in November 1992 (the year the building opened), Cawker says that the building's weightlessness, transparency, and lightness seem to have attracted most interest. She describes the building as having a "spidery sense of tectonics" and a "motif of sliding planes." She characterizes the approach to the building as an "unwinding coil," and writes, "arriving at the plateau of the site [from Moatfield Road], visitors ascend . . . and while climbing alternatively experience views back toward the long green ribbon of the Don Valley parkland and forward toward the folded space of the reception canopy, beyond that to the double height gallery, and beyond that through the clerestory to the pure landscape of the sky. . . "

Without requiring agreement, these words provide a useful introduction to one of the city's very interesting buildings from the late twentieth century.

PARC DOWNSVIEW PARK

35, 40, 65, and 75
Carl Hall Road (at Sheppard and Keele)

In 1929 the de Havilland Aircraft Company and its thirty-five employees moved here and occupied the building known as Plant 1, designed by the Toronto architects Mathers and Haldenby. The company had been manufacturing the Moth biplane, and was experimenting with different variations. In 1937, after de Havilland had grown considerably and Plant 1 had seen several additions, the Tiger Moth had its first test flight. It became the basic training plane for the Royal Canadian Air Force, and eventually fifteen hundred Tiger Moths were manufactured here.

With the coming of the Second World War, de Havilland began manufacturing the Mosquito aircraft—its fuselage was plywood, which

Photo of de Havilland Aircraft of Canada, shortly after moving to the Downsview site in 1929.

made the plane both light and fast—at a rate of three planes every two days. The Hangar building at 75 Carl Hall Road was constructed for this purpose in 1940. Following the war, the principal plane manufactured here was the CS2F-2 Tracker, an anti-submarine patrol plane. The company also specialized in short-takeoff-and-landing planes such as the Otter, the Beaver, and the Buffalo.

The Royal Canadian Air Force established itself on site and significantly expanded the land mass of the facility. In 1951 it built the enormous Supply Depot (40 Carl Hall Road), containing one million square feet of floor space. Since this building was used to supply mem-

Female war workers at de Havilland in 1940.

Inside the de Havilland plant, 1929.

bers of the North Atlantic Treaty Organization, it was designed with rein-forced concrete and a waffle-roofed ceiling to be atomic bomb–proof.

De Havilland has since been purchased by Bombardier, and it con-tinues to manufacture airplanes here, mostly the Dash 8, wings for the Learjet 45, and the Global Express corporate jet. The runway was sold by the Canadian government to de Havilland and is used for these new planes. Following its reorganization by the Department of National Defence, Canadian Forces moved from this base and closed it in 1996.

The buildings are clearly industrial in nature, with high ceilings, large, unobstructed floor space, plenty of glass, and little decoration. They now see other uses than those they were originally designed for. Plant 1 at 65 Carl Hall Road is now the Aerospace Museum Building, displaying a number of commercial, mili-tary, and experimental planes. Many volun-teers re-create and restore older planes, including Tiger Moths, and what may be Canada's most famous plane, the Avro Arrow, which the Canadian government decided not to support in the 1950s. The Hangar at 75 Carl Hall Road is used during the winter months as an indoor soccer facility, and as a trade show venue for the remainder of the year. The mammoth Supply Depot at 40

Farms were established in this area in the first third of the nineteenth century. Because of its high eleva-tion and its view toward Lake Ontario, John Perkins Bull's farm was apparently called Downs View—hence the name Downsview for this part of the city.

Carl Hall Road serves as studio for filming movies. The aircraft workshop built in 1952 is now used as the Parc Downsview Park corporate office (35 Carl Hall Road).

Since the Canadian armed forces no longer use this site, the government has been looking for a more appropriate use for the land. In the mid-1990s, a large theme park and entertainment complex was vociferously opposed by the community but endorsed by a majority of politicians, until the proponent walked away, claiming he was not receiving enough financial and other support. The more recent proposal is to treat as an urban park much of the vast publicly owned space to the west of the railway tracks bisecting the site. An international competition was undertaken at considerable expense (on the order of $5 million was spent), with the winning plan proposing to encourage natural growth on most of the site and denser plantings and sports fields on the remainder. Called Tree City, the design calls for 25 per cent of the site to be forest and for the creation of a thousand crossing paths for joggers, cyclists, and pedestrians. Implementation of this design is to proceed in 2002 or 2003.

The main impression this area imparts is vastness of scale—at 644 acres the site is exceptionally large. One reason is that most of the land is empty; another is that unlike the rest of the city, the site is not broken up by roads into smaller, more comprehensible chunks; a third is the site's high elevation, allowing a good view over the city. It's rare to find such a vantage point in the middle of an urban area.

Aerial view of Downsview Park today, Canada's first national urban park.

WINDFIELDS
(CANADIAN FILM CENTRE)

 2489 Bayview Avenue

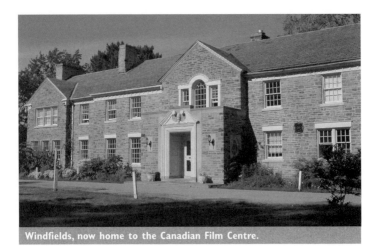

Windfields, now home to the Canadian Film Centre.

E. P. (Edward Plunkett) Taylor was perhaps Canada's best-known businessman in the twentieth century. He was born in Ottawa in 1901, began working with the McLeod Young Weir investment firm in the 1920s, and came to Toronto in 1929. The next year he formed the company that became known as Canadian Breweries, which made many of Canada's most popular beers, including O'Keefe. By the mid-1930s Taylor was wealthy enough to want a large country home where he could pursue his interests in racehorses, and he established Windfields Farm.

Taylor was one of the famous "dollar-a-year" men (they were paid that amount for working full-time in the war effort) recruited during the Second World War by C. D. Howe, a minister in the federal government, and he worked on supply issues with the Americans and then the British. After the war he formed the Argus Corporation as a holding company. He led the development of the land on the west side of Bayview, including the creation of York Mills Plaza, one of the earliest shopping plazas in the city. He purchased more than two thousand acres of farmland to the east and undertook the most influential suburban development in North America, Don Mills, in the early 1950s. With its curving streets, wide house lots, separated uses, central shopping plaza, and extraordinary financial success, Don Mills created the style that suburban subdivisions have followed ever since. Taylor also established the business approach to suburban land development that is now common practice: in exchange for being given a relatively free hand in deciding how land would be developed, he assumed all financial risk that previously was borne by the municipality. This too was a legacy of Don Mills.

In the early 1960s he sponsored a new performing space in the city at Front and Yonge Streets, the O'Keefe Centre, now known as the Hummingbird Centre. He was an active member of the Ontario Jockey Club and most successful as a breeder, producing many famous racehorses, including Northern Dancer and Nijinksi. He died in 1989.

Taylor and his wife, Winnifred, commissioned this building in 1936 as a home for themselves and their young children but with a style suited to their financial and social prominence. Designed in the American Colonial Revival style, this was the first substantial house in an area now crowded with estate-type properties, particularly to the southeast. The fieldstone, the white pediment over the entrance, and the curving driveway all have an appropriate grandeur, as does the breadth of the building, yet inside, the main theme is more family comfort than social entertaining. The twenty-two-acre grounds are impressive—tennis courts, a pool, a pleasant garden, a small stable. The white fences mark an estate to be noticed.

In 1986 Taylor gave the property to the city, and it was been used since 1988 by the Canadian Film Centre, founded by Canada's most famous movie maker, Norman Jewison. The Centre provides essential training in film, video, and new media for Canadians and has established a strong reputation among film directors and producers throughout the world. The Centre's presence accounts for film memorabilia throughout the building.

E. P. Taylor at home in Windfields, 1941 (CTA SC266.71562).

ZION CHURCH CULTURAL CENTRE
(ZION PRIMITIVE METHODIST CHURCH)

1650 Finch Avenue East

This is the highest point of land in Toronto—an appropriate place for a religious institution, even if today it does seem stranded by the wide roadway in front and the suburban development to all sides. Before the first log church was constructed here in the mid-1800s, the site was well used by aboriginal Canadians, as the artifacts dug up when the addition was constructed in the late 1990s indicate.

The current church was built in 1873 for a Methodist congregation and has similarities to other modest country churches in Upper Canada of the time, with small hints of grandeur—yellow brick is added to the red for decoration, strong buttresses line the walls, a pleasant belfry sits over the main entrance, and there are tall chimneys. Inside, one can see where the stovepipes ran close to the ceiling to provide a modicum of warmth in the bleak winters. The original tongue-and-groove pine floors attest to the existence of large trees, now entirely lumbered from this area. The beaded wainscotting shows a nice decorative touch. The two stained-glass windows were probably installed in the early twentieth century. A few examples of the original pews remain, but the space has generally been cleared for the community programs that now find a home here.

The congregation came from the farms in the surrounding L'Amoreaux community (named after one of the earliest families to settle in the area), but in the twentieth century numbers had declined to such an extent that by mid-century the building sat vacant and boarded up. It was probably the cemetery that saved the church from demolition as suburbia rolled through the community in the 1960s and '70s. Digging up and relocating 130 graves is big trouble for any developer. The first markers show burials in the 1850s, but some may have occurred earlier. The cemetery is now generally closed to further burials.

The property was designated in 1977 under the Ontario Heritage Act as a fine example of the Gothic Revival style, and then renovated. The rear addition was built in the late 1990s by the city to make the facility available for local use and programming.

The Zion Primitive Methodist Church, as this building was originally called, was built in 1873 by the Methodists of L'Amoreaux.

WEST

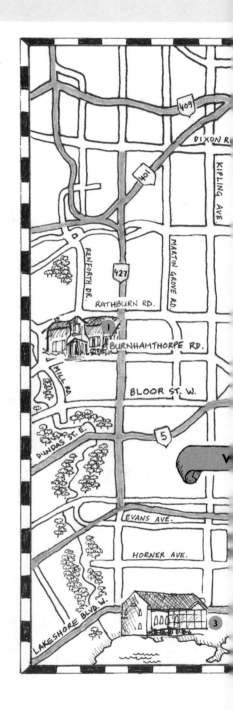

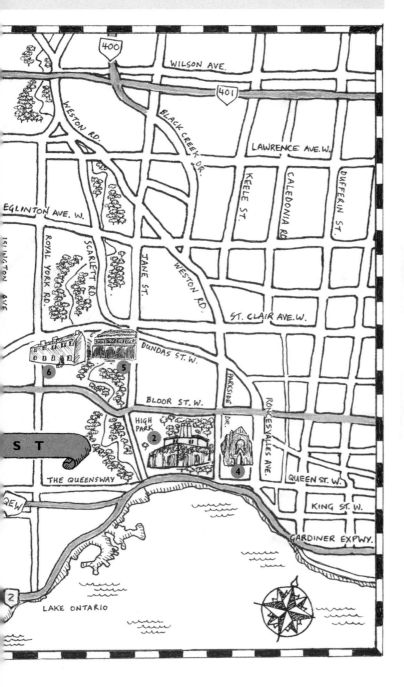

APPLEWOOD
(J. S. WOODSWORTH HOMESTEAD)

 450 The West Mall

James Shaver Woodsworth, the leading voice of his generation for social reform and often called "the conscience of Canada," was born in this house in 1874 and lived here until his parents moved the family to Portage la Prairie, Manitoba, eight years later. He travelled widely with his father, a Methodist preacher, and was himself ordained as a Methodist minister in 1896.

After two years of study at Oxford, he returned to Canada infused with the social gospel, decrying personal salvation in favour of social equity and the creation of the Kingdom of God on earth. He worked with poor immigrants in Winnipeg from 1904 until 1913, became active in the trade union movement, was a declared pacifist in the Great War, and opposed conscription. He finally resigned from his ministry because of the Church's support for the war.

Woodsworth was active in the Winnipeg General Strike in 1919 and was arrested for sedition because of editorials he wrote supporting the strike, but the charges were never proceeded with. He was elected to Parliament in 1921 on the platform "Human Needs Before Property

Rights." He was a vigorous organizer for social equity and played the critical role in forcing Prime Minister Mackenzie King to introduce old-age pensions in 1927. He helped organize the Regina Conference in 1933 that saw the creation of a new political party, the Co-operative Commonwealth Federation—three decades later it became the New Democratic Party—and was its first leader. Seven CCFers were elected to Parliament in 1935, including Tommy Douglas. Woodsworth continued in Parliament to express his pacifist views and opposed the declaration of war in 1939. He was re-elected in 1940 and died in 1942.

The building that was the first home to this exceptional Canadian is a pleasant, modest brick farmhouse, constructed in 1851 in a vernacular Georgian style, with the front porch adding a touch of grace. It was originally located at the northeast corner of Burnhamthorpe and the West Mall, but when a developer proposed destruction of the building in 1980 for a new office complex, it was rescued by active citizens after Etobicoke City Council disclaimed any interest.

The house faces south, sideways to the street, so that it reveals its side and tail to the passing traffic, thereby reflecting the strange character of the West Mall. Virtually every building on this thoroughfare makes a point of demeaning the street by locating the main entrance off a parking lot or to the side. In the denser and more compact city, one function of buildings is to emphasize the street edge; here in the suburbs, planners have gone to considerable lengths to make the street edge as invisible and uninteresting as possible; conse-quently, there is little to attract one's attention here. If a "mall" is a street meant for pedestrians, this is something of a misnomer.

Inside, the house is pleasantly furnished in an early-twentieth-century style. The private foun-dation responsible for maintain-ing the building generates most of its revenue from wedding rentals. A doll collection has been donated for safekeeping and is stored here. Items from the col-lection are often put on display.

J. S. Woodsworth (1874–1942) was the best known of the reform-minded Social Gospel ministers.

COLBORNE LODGE

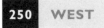 High Park

This photo was taken during the 1920s, shortly after the Women's Canadian Historical Society restored the house for the public.

John Howard and his wife, Jemima, came to Canada from England in 1832. As a trained architect he quickly found work, first as a drawing master at Upper Canada College, then as surveyor to Toronto in 1834. In 1836 he purchased 160 acres for his country home, which was constructed in 1837 and occupied on December 23. He named it after his patron, Lieutenant-Governor Sir John Colborne, who had returned to England the previous year.

He designed the house in a Regency style with dominant French doors and an expansive bay window open to the bright southern exposure, ringed by a wide veranda—the building's main room opens to the garden and the park. The front door is inconspicuously placed on the west side of the building. Perhaps this was done to permit a direct connection between the main living space and the natural world, a kind of romantic touch. The house had a magnificent view over the lake, now at a considerable distance to the south because of landfill, and the quiet that Howard would have experienced is broken by the relentless roar of the expressway to the south and an occasional passing train.

John Howard (1803–1890) was an architect and surveyor who designed a number of important buildings in Toronto, including the Mental Asylum at 999 Queen Street West (demolished in the 1970s) and St. John's Anglican Church, York Mills. He also, created the plan for the St. James' Cemetery on Parliament Street. When his wife died in 1877, he designed and erected a monument for her in a plot just west of the house, which he surrounded by an iron fence from St. Paul's Cathedral in London. When he died in 1890, he too was buried there.

At the heart of the structure is the tall three-part chimney, providing fireplaces for the living room, the kitchen (which over time became a dining room), and a bedroom. A few years after occupying the house, Howard added a second floor and several rooms on the north side, and in 1855 he and his wife made it their principal residence year-round. The interior remains decorated in a mid-nineteenth-century style, as Howard would have experienced it. Several of his watercolours hang in the house.

Howard made several attempts to subdivide his large property around the house, without success. In 1872, as pressures grew for more civic parkland, he transferred his 160 acres to the City in return for an annuity payable until his death. The City added other lands at later dates to create today's High Park, about 400 acres in size.

The Coach House contains artifacts original to John Howard. Here we see a one-horse carriage called a phaeton, designed for a woman in formal dress to enter and exit with ease. The boat has a place for two sets of oars and a sail; the Howards took it out on Grenadier Pond.

HUMBER COLLEGE, LAKESHORE CAMPUS

3131 Lakeshore Boulevard West

The grandest and most successful attempt to impose order on a large field of space in the Toronto area is probably this complex of nine red-brick buildings. They were built by the provincial government as the Mimico (Mental) Asylum in the last decade of the nineteenth century, and the architect was Kivas Tully. Since 1867, Tully had been the architect and engineer in the provincial Department of Public Works. He is credited with designing Toronto's first sewer system.

Tully attempted a design that departed from the massive approach of the Mental Asylum (999 Queen Street West) toward a more intimate treatment facility for the mentally ill, making use of smaller buildings. Twenty years later, a further iteration of this kind of thinking resulted in the cottages found in the Whitby Mental Hospital: here at Mimico, the design reached a halfway point, and the patients were lodged in rather grand houses.

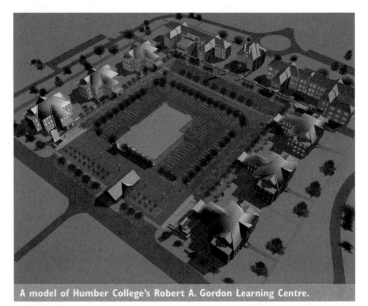

A model of Humber College's Robert A. Gordon Learning Centre.

The eleven buildings were carefully placed around a central quadrangle, with the westerly side left open. The most easterly houses have been joined to their neighbours, so today it appears as though there are just nine separate structures. Nor are the houses exactly as they were built. Front porches have been removed,

One of several "cottages" in the Lakeshore Psychiatric Hospital complex, built by the provincial government in the late nineteenth century.

and wings (decorated with stucco) have been tastefully added, probably in the 1920s. A more recent change to the buildings on the north side of the quadrangle is the louvred wooden porticos.

Except for the keystone structure, the buildings all have a common roofline and a common eaves-line, lending serenity and continuity. The same Georgian multi-paned window shape is used throughout, and it has a fine sense of proportion. Each roof sports a finial much like a feather in a cap. Only the keystone structure—the central building on the east side—differs. It is a half-storey higher than the others, with tall chimneys, and a pediment bracketed by turrets over a triptych of windows. (A tower has since been removed.) It provides a strong focal point for the quadrangle.

The edge of the quadrangle is defined by a raised walkway that acts like the edge of a bowl to the central portion of the quadrangle. The walkway has recently been refurbished in brick, with a handsome brick-and-stone parapet, and disguises the fact it serves as a roof of what was once a tunnel permitting food to be delivered from a central commissary to the patients living in the houses.

Several changes have been made that denigrate Tully's grand plan. A two-storey administrative building was plunked into the centre of the quadrangle in the 1960s, and it proves an ugly distraction. It is surrounded by parking and loading bays and, more recently, a ring road. New chimneys for steam and smoke have been erected just in front of the keystone building in apparent disregard of Tully's careful attempt to provide graceful focus.

The asylum functioned here until the early 1990s, when it was closed and the site became vacant. In 1994 Humber College was given a long lease on the property, and the slow process of conversion and restoration is now under way. Several buildings on the north side of the quadrangle are now in use as classrooms.

ASSEMBLY HALL 3121 Lakeshore Boulevard West

To the northwest of the quadrangle is the building that served as the place of both recreation and worship for the residents of the asylum. Built in 1897, it is in style very similar to the buildings around the quadrangle—red brick, pitched roof, well-proportioned windows. It feels like a great big schoolhouse.

This building—now the Lakeshore Community Cultural Centre—has been renovated by the architect Stephen Teeple, and a new entry facility has been added in a Modern style that effectively enhances the old, with its contrasting materials of glass and aluminum, and crispness of line. Inside is a 220-seat performance hall, exhibition space, and meeting rooms, providing a much needed centre for arts, heritage, and cultural activity in the area.

THE GATEHOUSE 3101 Lakeshore Boulevard West

The original entrance to the asylum was from Lakeshore Boulevard, to the east of the quadrangle (not the present extension of Kipling Avenue, which is relatively recent), and this house stood at this entrance as the gatehouse. Built in 1910, it is a two-storey brick cottage with attractive porches at the front and side. Originally, it was the home of the doctor on staff at the asylum. After being vacant for many decades, it has recently been renovated to serve as a centre for abused children.

Landscaping was an important element in the original design of the asylum, and it began here, at the main entrance to the grounds on the roadway that leads to the east side of the keystone building. It consisted of large trees along the roadway, many shrubs, and tended gardens. The gardener, Samuel Matheson, lived on site to tend the plantings. Sadly, little remains of this element of the design.

To return to the walkway around the quadrangle for one final moment: the view of the lake to the south over what was once a cricket field remains enchanting. The proportion and detailing of the buildings around the complex provide an enticing picture of ordered calm that Tully intended to create on this land.

JAMI MOSQUE

56 Boustead Avenue

There is no question this First World War–era building was erected as a Presbyterian church: hardy red brick, modified Gothic arches over the main door, a stubby tower never intended to sport a spire, which would be too unrestrained. But by mid-century,

the church was losing its Protestant congregation, never to return, and instead gained Muslim worshippers. In 1968 the building became the first mosque in the Toronto area to serve the growing number of Muslims.

The structure has undergone little physical change; indeed, only the Arabic script of the exterior signs makes it clear that the building has experienced the same kind of faith transformation that has happened to several other places of workshop in Toronto. Inside, the pews have been removed to create a large, open room that has been fully carpeted but otherwise is devoid of decoration—there are no religious artifacts or imagery. Since Muslims pray toward Mecca (in Canada, facing the east), this structure is inappropriate in its north/south orientation, and one notes that those praying do so toward the east wall of the building.

As in other mosques, a separate entry is provided for both men and women. Shoes must be removed before worshippers approach the sanctuary.

Inside Jami Mosque.

LAMBTON HOUSE

4066 Old Dundas Street

Today, Lambton House is a bit like a fish out of water, but there was a time when it was smack in the middle of things. This section of Dundas Street marks one of the first bridges over the Humber River, built in 1810, a bridge that stood until 1954, when Hurricane Hazel washed away its approaches and it was dismantled.

Lambton House was built for William Pearce Howland in 1848. Howland was an entrepreneur, investing in railways and land, and sponsored the School for the Deaf in Cobourg. As a Reform politician, he was elected to the Legislature in 1858 and was involved in the meetings that led to the confederation of Canadian provinces in 1867. He served as lieutenant-governor for Ontario from 1868 to 1873 and was knighted shortly thereafter.

Howland owned Lambton Mills, which stood across the street where a yellow-brick apartment building is now found. The mill office and general store were immediately to the west of Lambton House. Howland's home was up the hill, slightly to the north. As well as being a hotel and tavern, Lambton House was something of a transportation

The Lambton House Hotel (shown circa 1860) served continuously as a tavern and hotel for 140 years.

hub, since Old Dundas Street was then the main route west from Toronto. Stagecoaches stopped right in front of the building (the current lawn is a recent change—the veranda used to open directly onto the road), and the Lambton Street railway, powered from a generating plant on the Humber River, turned around on the road in front. This was also a route to the Carrying Place, the pathway (or portage, since everything had to be carried between two water courses) on the east side of the Humber eventually leading north over the Oak Ridges Moraine to a water connection to Georgian Bay.

In 1915 a spring flood washed out the dam on the Humber. That same year the mill that had been purchased by the property developer Home Smith and converted into a restaurant and theatre burned down. Several years later, the building that had served as the mill office and general store also burned down. In 1928 the city built the high-level crossing of the river—the new Dundas Street—just to the north, in the process demolishing Howland's house. The latter half of the twentieth century was no more kind, with the local politicians agreeing to an ungainly apartment building in the backyard of Lambton House and townhouses to the east that are no more sympathetic.

Lambton House—a simple brick structure made impressive by the two-storey veranda—was probably built by William Tyrrell, responsible for most other Howland structures. Inside, the staircase is original, from 1858, with hand-turned spindles. Several window sashes, doorframes, and some plaster work also date from that period. A portrait of Sir William hangs in the Howland Room. The building functioned as a tavern until 1988, when the complaints of surrounding residents grew loud, and it has since been protected by vigilant heritage buffs who are coaxing the City into investing in the building's improvement (sprinklers have been installed). They sponsor community activities like pub and euchre nights to generate operating funds. It's clear the structure needs all the support and attention it can get.

The Lambton name is often applied to this area of the city. It comes from John George Lambton, Lord Durham, author of the Durham Report, which is said to have established responsible government in the Canadas. Durham also signed the popular Rebellion Losses Bill, which saw the public purse compensating families for losses suffered in the Rebellion of 1837.

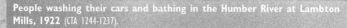

People washing their cars and bathing in the Humber River at Lambton Mills, 1922 (CTA 1244-1237).

MONTGOMERY'S INN

4709 Dundas Street West

The name is the same, but this is not the Montgomery's Tavern where the rebels gathered in December 1837 for their ill-fated uprising—that tavern was on Yonge Street north of Eglinton. This inn, owned by Thomas Montgomery, was built about 1830.

Montgomery was born in Ireland in 1790 and before coming to Canada in 1815 worked in the salt trade and as a surveyor. In Canada he was a successful farmer, and the farm produce fed the staff and visitors at the inn. (Inside, in the back stairwell, is a sign from the mid-nineteenth century showing a farmer, a plough, and a team, and the house was known "by the sign of the plough.") The inn met with enough success to be expanded in 1838 by two further window bays on the eastern side (which explains why the door no longer centres the facade) and a large room at the rear. Like Lambton House a few miles to the east, this hotel was on the well-travelled road to Dundas (which was much more prosperous than Hamilton because of its mills) and beside a water crossing, in this case Mimico Creek.

This building, one of Ontario's finest remaining examples of Loyalist Georgian architecture, was erected about 1830.

The quarry stone now so visible was once covered with pebble-dash (stucco is our current name for the material) and the corners of this Georgian-style building were enhanced to appear to be blocks of cut stone. Note the modest fanlight above the main door. It is possible that the roadway was located much closer to the main door, and that the lawn and small retaining wall were added after the relocation and the widening of Dundas Street in the twentieth century to accommodate a much more significant bridge over the creek.

Inside, the building has been well restored to a style of the 1850s. The tall case clock in the main hallway is said to have belonged to the Montgomerys. The bar on the main floor

is caged in a style of the period. Upstairs is the ballroom, and the Montgomerys' bedroom, which is relatively fancy compared with other rooms. Innkeepers were required to provide two clean beds: this inn provided three private bedrooms.

The inn prospered until rail travel became popular in the 1850s, when it promptly went out of business. Thomas Montgomery died here in 1877, but the building remained in the family until 1945. In the 1960s a developer purchased it, but the City refused to provide the inn protection, and the Etobicoke Historical Society was forced to raise funds to purchase it. In 1967 the City of Etobicoke was persuaded to fund its renovation as a Centennial project: new casements were supplied for the windows, and somewhat inexplicably, a decision was made to strip the pebble-dash from the exterior, thus exposing the quarry stone for the first time in the building's long life. Since then, Montgomery's Inn has become established as an important and interesting museum in the city's west end.

BIBLIOGRAPHY

The most useful books to begin exploring Toronto's physical history are the following:

- Arthur, Eric. *Toronto, No Mean City*, third edition revised by Stephen A. Otto. University of Toronto Press, 1986. This book is about the architecture of nineteenth-century Toronto and is full of lively anecdotes and opinions and excellent illustrations.

- Dendy, William, and William Kilbourn. *Toronto Observed, Its Architecture, Patrons and History*. Oxford University Press, Toronto, 1986. This book tells the social and architectural stories of about seventy-five buildings or groups of building.

- Gatenby, Greg. *Toronto: A Literary Guide*. McArthur & Company, Toronto, 1999. This is a treasure trove of information about the city's literary history, noting street addresses where authors lived, wrote, spoke, and partied.

- McHugh, Patricia. *Toronto Architecture: A City Guide*, second edition. McClelland & Stewart, 1989. An architectural guide to the central city, listing architects, dates of construction, often including a photo, and a small description of the structure.

OTHER INTERESTING AND HELPFUL BOOKS ABOUT TORONTO'S HERITAGE INCLUDE:

- Ardiel, June. *Sculpture/Toronto: An Illustrated Guide to Toronto's Historic and Contemporary Sculpture*. Toronto: Leidra Books, 1994.

- The Bureau of Architecture and Urbanism. *Toronto Modern Architecture 1945–65*. Toronto: The Coach House Press, 1987.

- Darke, Eleanor. *"A Mill Should Be Built Thereon": An Early*

History of the Todmorden Mills. Toronto: Natural History/Natural Heritage Inc., 1995.

- Dendy, William. *Lost Toronto.* Toronto: Oxford University Press, 1978.

- Dieterman, Frank A., and Ronald F. Williamson. *Government on Fire: The History and Archaeology of Upper Canada's First Parliament Buildings.* Toronto: eastendbooks, an imprint of Venture Press, 2001.

- Fulford, Robert. *Accidental City: The Transformation of Toronto.* Toronto: Macfarlane Walter & Ross, 1995.

- Jeffreys, Peter. *George Greek Orthodox Church: An Architectural and Iconographic Guide.* Toronto: St. George's Greek Orthodox Church, 2000

- Kalman, Harold. *A History of Canadian Architecture.* Toronto: Oxford University Press, 1994.

- Kilbourn, William. *Intimate Grandeur: One Hundred Years at Massey Hall.* Toronto: Stoddart, 1993.

- Lundell, Liz. *The Estates of Old Toronto.* Erin Mills, Ont.: Boston Mills Press, 1997.

- Mays, John Bentley. *Emerald City.* Toronto: Viking, 1994.

- McKelvey, Margaret and Merilyn. *Toronto Carved in Stone.* Toronto: Fitzhenry & Whiteside, 1984.

- Richardson, Douglas, with J. M. S. Careless, G. M. Craig and Peter Heyworth. *A Not Unsightly Building: University College and Its History.* Oakville: Mosaic Press, 1990.

- Sisier, Rebecca. *Art for Enlightenment.* Toronto: Learnx Foundation, Toronto Board of Education, Fitzhenry & Whiteside, 1993.

- Speisman, Stephen A. *The Jews of Toronto: A History to 1937.* Toronto: McClelland & Stewart, 1979.

- The Spencer Clark Collection of Historic Architecture. *The Guild.* Toronto: The Guild, n.d.

TORONTO PUBLIC LIBRARY BOOKLETS:

- Campbell, Mary, and Barbara Myrvold. *The Beach in Pictures, 1793–1932.*

- Campbell, Mary, and Barbara Myrvold. *Historical Walking Tour of Kew Beach.*

- Forsyth, Barbara, and Barbara Myrvold. *The Most Attractive Resort in Town: Public Library Service in West Toronto Junction, 1888–1989.*

- Hutcheson, Stephanie. *Yorkville in Pictures, 1853 to 1883.*

- Laycock, Margaret, and Barbara Myrvold. *Parkdale in Pictures, Its Development to 1889.*

- Moon, Lynda, Barbara Myrvold, and Elizabeth Ridler. *Historical Walking Tour of Lawrence Park.*

- Myrvold, Barbara. *Historical Walking Tour of the Danforth.*

- Myrvold, Barbara. *Historical Walking Tour of Kensington Market and College Street.*

- Patterson, Cynthia, Carol McDougall, and George Levin. *Bloor–Dufferin in Pictures.*

⬚ ACKNOWLEDGMENTS

My thanks to Margie Zeidler who suggested my name for this project; to Stephen Otto for helpful historical advice; and to the many curators and others responsible for buildings discussed in this book. My appreciation also goes to Allison Savaria for her research support and index preparation and to the superb work of editor Noelle Zitzer (particularly for gathering photos) and copy editor Alison Reid.

Doors Open Toronto is a program of the City of Toronto Culture Division, in co-operation with Heritage Toronto, the Toronto Heritage and Culture Foundation, the Toronto Historical Association, the Toronto Society of Architects, and St. Lawrence Works. Doors Open Toronto is presented by *The Toronto Star,* with support from CBC Radio One, CBC Television, Diamante Development Corporation, Taylor/Hazell Architects Ltd., and Clifford Restoration Limited. For Doors Open information, contact the Culture Division at 416 338 0628, or *www.doorsopen.org.*

Heritage Toronto is a citizen-based organization in Toronto's heritage movement, and those interested are encouraged to become members, both to participate in events it sponsors and to become aware of political activity around protecting heritage structures in Toronto. It can be contacted at 416 338 0684 or *www.heritagetoronto.org.*

John Sewell, the author of this book, is interested in making contact with those interested in heritage preservation. His e-mail address is *j.sewell@on.aibn.com.*

ILLUSTRATION CREDITS

Every reasonable effort has been made to trace ownership of copyright materials. Information enabling the Publisher to rectify any reference or credit in future editions will be welcomed.

BOOK COVER (front, left to right): R. C. Harris Filtration Plant © 2001 Deirdre Molina; Elgin Theatre, courtesy of the Ontario Heritage Foundation; Commerce Court North, courtesy of the City of Toronto Culture Division; Liberty Grand, courtesy of Liberty Entertainment Group

SPINE (top to bottom): One King West, courtesy of the City of Toronto Culture Division; Humber College, courtesy of Taylor/Hazell Architects Ltd.; Winter Garden Theatre, courtesy of the Ontario Heritage Foundation

MAPS © 2002 Charles Checketts, charleschecketts@hotmail.com

p. 2 Kevin Hewitt/Clifford Restoration Limited; pp. 3–4 © 2002 Neil Graham; p. 5 the Arts and Letters Club; p. 6 © 2002 Neil Graham; p. 7 © Design Archive/Burley, used by permission of Brookfield Properties Ltd.; p.8 Kevin Hewitt/Clifford Restoration Limited; p. 9 © Design Archive/Burley, used by permission of Brookfield Properties Ltd.; pp. 11–12 © 2002 Neil Graham; p. 13 © 2002 Ron Gaudet; p. 15 Toronto Public Library (MTRL T32455); p. 16 City of Toronto Archives 1244-3181; p. 17 City of Toronto Culture Division; p. 18 CIBC Archives, Toronto; p. 19 © 2002 Neil Graham; p. 21 Liberty Entertainment Group; p. 22 City of Toronto Archives SC231-1668; p. 23 © 2002 Neil Graham; p. 24 (top) © 2002 Neil Graham; p. 24 (bottom) City of Toronto Archives 1244-144; p. 25 du Toit Allsopp Hillier; pp. 27–29 Ontario Heritage Foundation; p. 30 Fairmont Royal York Hotel; p. 31 (top) Fairmont Royal York Hotel; p. 31 (bottom) Archives of Ontario I0002051; p. 32 Fairmont Royal York Hotel; pp. 33–34 City of Toronto Culture Division; p. 35 Tippin Corporation; pp. 36–38 © 2002 Neil Graham; p. 39 Panda Associates 60977-50, reproduced by permission of Hummingbird Centre for the

Performing Arts Corporation; pp. 40–41 Victoria College; p. 43 City of Toronto Culture Division; p. 44 National Archives of Canada (Imperial Oil Collection) C-013988; p. 45 Collection of the Corporation of the City of Toronto; p. 46 City of Toronto Archives SC231-98; p. 47 City of Toronto Archives 1983-121-4; City of Toronto Archives SC246-49; p. 49 City of Toronto Culture Division; p. 50 Archives of Ontario I0001871; p. 51 © Alan Scharf; p. 52 Archives of Ontario I0001872; p. 53 © Avril Hill, used by permission of the Metropolitan United Church; pp. 54–55 Moriyama & Teshima; p. 56 City of Toronto, Media Services; p. 57 © Steven Evans; p. 59 City of Toronto, Media Services; p. 60 Toronto Public Library (MTRL pc2708); p. 61 (top) City of Toronto Culture Division; p. 61 (bottom) Toronto Public Library (MTRL T10258); p. 62 (top) © Steven Evans; p. 62 (bottom) City of Toronto Archives 1244-323; p. 63 City of Toronto Archives 1244-323M; pp. 64 and 65 (top) City of Toronto Culture Division; p. 65 (bottom) One King West/Stinson Properties Inc.; p. 66. City of Toronto Archives 1244-1086; p. 67 Ontario Heritage Foundation; pp. 68–69) City of Toronto Culture Division; p. 70 City of Toronto Archives 1244-1131; p. 71 Toronto Public Library (MTRL T10058); p. 72 City of Toronto Archives 1244-3153; p. 73 Kevin Hewitt/Clifford Restoration Limited; p. 74 City of Toronto Culture Division; p. 75 City of Toronto Archives 1244-310); p. 76 © 2002 Neil Graham; p. 77 Liberty Entertainment Group; pp. 78–80 Le Royal Meridien King Edward Hotel; pp. 81–82 © 2002 Neil Graham; p. 83 Archives of Ontario I0001846; Toronto Public Library (MTRL T10740); pp. 85–87 © 2002 Neil Graham; pp. 88–89 Archives of Ontario I0005329; pp. 90–91 Citizens for the Old Town; p. 92 TD Bank Financial Group: Archives Dept.; p. 93 Toronto Public Library (MTRL pc1369); p. 94 Toronto–Dominion Bank Archives; p. 96 City of Toronto Archives 1244-3178; p. 97 © 2002 Neil Graham; p. 98 Kevin Hewitt/Clifford Restoration Limited; p. 99 Toronto Terminals Railway Company Ltd.; pp. 100–101 photos provided by Ontario Realty Corporation; pp. 104–105 © Steven Evans, used by permission of A. J. Diamond, Donald Schmitt and Company; p. 106 © Fiona Spalding Smith, used by permission of A. J. Diamond, Donald Schmitt and Company; pp. 108–109 Canadian Opera Company; p. 110 © 2002 Ron Gaudet; p. 111 (both) © 2002 Neil Graham; p. 112 © 2002 Gregg Taylor; p. 113 City of Toronto

Archives 1244-306; pp. 114–115 © Ron Jack; pp. 116–118 © 2002 Neil Graham; p. 119 (top) © 2002 Ron Gaudet; p. 119 (bottom) Toronto Public Library (MTRL T30358); p. 120 Jarvis Collegiate; pp. 121, 123, 125–129 © 2002 Neil Graham; p. 131 City of Toronto Culture Division; p. 135 © 2002 Neil Graham; pp. 136–137 reproduced by permission of *The Toronto Star*; p. 139, City of Toronto Archives 1244-3172; p. 140 City of Toronto Archives 1244-116; p. 141 City of Toronto Culture Division; pp. 142–143 courtesy Taylor/Hazell Architects Ltd.; p. 145 Toronto Public Library (MTRL S1-735B); pp. 146–147 © 2002 Noelle Zitzer; p. 148 © 2002 Neil Graham; p. 149 © 2002 Ron Gaudet; pp. 150–152 José San Juan/City of Toronto Culture Division; p. 153–155 401 Richmond; p. 156 (top) Ontario Heritage Foundation; p. 156 (bottom) National Archives of Canada C-026415; p. 157 Ontario Heritage Foundation; p. 158 © 2002 Neil Graham; pp. 160–161 © 2002 Gregg Taylor; p. 162 City of Toronto Archives 1244-2150; pp. 164–166 © 2002 Neil Graham; p. 167 Toronto Public Library (MTRL T33418); pp. 168–169 City of Toronto Archives 1244-2024; p. 170 Liberty Entertainment Group; p. 171 © 2002 Gregg Taylor; p. 172 Mirvish Productions; pp. 173–174 Roy Thomson Hall/City of Toronto Culture Division; p. 175 © 2002 Neil Graham; pp. 176–177 Mirvish Productions; pp. 178–179 © 2002 Gregg Taylor; p. 181 © 2002 Ron Gaudet; p. 182 National Archives of Canada PA-137052; p. 183 © Bruce Litteljohn; p. 184 © Cat O'Neil, used by permission of St. Anne's Anglican Church; p. 185 City of Toronto Culture Division; p. 186 © Don Cooper, used by permission of the City of Toronto Culture Division; p. 187 Toronto Public Library (MTRL T31037); p. 188 City of Toronto Culture Division; p. 189 (top) National Archives of Canada PA-167890; p. 189 (bottom) Steam Whistle Brewing; p. 190 Toronto Carpet Factory; pp. 192–193 © 2002 Neil Graham; p. 193 Archives of Ontario I0002056; p. 195 Toronto Public Library (MTRL T13147); p. 196 City of Toronto Archives 1244-3144; p. 197 Toronto Public Library (MTRL T13151); pp. 198–199 City of Toronto Archives 1244-752; p. 201 © 2002 Gregg Taylor; pp. 202–203 © 2002 Ron Gaudet; p. 206 © 2002 Neil Graham; p. 208 © 2002 Ron Gaudet; p. 209 City of Toronto Archives 1244-1152; p. 210 City of Toronto Culture Division; p. 211 Toronto Police Museum; pp. 212–216 © 2002 Ron Gaudet; p. 217 Kevin Hewitt/Clifford Restoration Limited; pp. 218–220 © 2002 Ron

🚪 INDEX

Bold type indicates main entry